1.99

Old Bi

i

The Spirit of the Man

Stephen Lowe

Methuen Drama

Published by Methuen 2005

1 3 5 7 9 10 8 6 4 2

First published in 2005 by
Methuen Publishing Limited
11–12 Buckingham Gate
London SW1E 6LB

Reprinted with revisions in 2005

Copyright © 2005 Stephen Lowe

Stephen Lowe has asserted his rights under
the Copyright, Designs and Patents Act, 1988,
to be identified as the author of this work

Methuen Publishing Limited Reg. No. 3543167

A CIP catalogue record for this book is available from
the British Library

ISBN 0 413 77538 0

Typeset by Country Setting, Kingsdown, Kent
Printed and bound in Great Britain by
Bookmarque Ltd, Croydon, Surrey

Nottingham Playhouse theatre company

presents

Old Big 'Ead in
The Spirit of the Man

by Stephen Lowe

First performance on Tuesday 7 June 2005
at Nottingham Playhouse.

Sponsored by

Insurance Brokers and Risk Managers

Presented in co-promotion with

**Championing
Nottinghamshire**

COVER IMAGE: original image supplied by JMS Photography, design by DE FACTO.

FOREWORD

Writing a play for Nottingham about Brian Clough is dangerously akin to premiering a piece about Pope John Paul II in Rome. Everyone here seems to have met him, knows everything about him, feels great affection towards him, and most of them feel they can do a pretty good imitation! Old Big 'Ead's memory is cherished here, as well as around the world. He was truly an inspirational figure, and it was this aspect of his character that, quite literally, inspired me - to write a play about INSPIRATION. Here was a man possessed by vision and sheer determination who lifted a group of not necessarily the greatest players in the world to, amongst other things, two successive European cups and lifted not only the spirit of my home town, and the whole country, but countless millions beyond who were fired by this meteoric rise. I remember being in St. Petersburg at the time of the second final and all the Russians knew of Nottingham was, well, they had heard of Robin Hood but the name on all their lips was the leader of another band of Merrie Men. And it's a name still to be conjured with, not only for the record achievements, but also for giving us sight of a different game, one to which many of us dream of returning - no casual long-balls, no time-wasting passing, no tirades against the ref, no hacking down of opponents, no star prima donnas. Just a team playing as one. Brian's boys played a beautiful as well as a successful game.

I never met him. Like most Forest supporters, I only saw him march out of the tunnel to the tune of "Robin Hood". Alan Dossor, the director of this show, and I used to travel to most of the key away games until Hillsborough, and that of course was another life experience - this time a tragic one - we all lived through in a way with Brian. As part of his band. All our lives were entwined around a patch of green. The old question of whether or not he was "the greatest manager England never had" can never be resolved now, but what we might at least agree on is that it would have been a lot more fun to see old Cloughie have a shot than some of the others who have worn the tie. Fun is not a word applied much to football nowadays (certainly not at the moment to his old team), but Brian had a sense of joy, and a load of laughs, that infected everyone whether football supporters or not. He always seemed to me, with his northern dry drawl, his deadpan expression, and his carefully honed use of almost Wildean epigrams, to be potentially "the greatest comedian England never had". I can't solve the riddle of the "English manager" question, but I have been so inspired by Old Big 'Ead to offer him the stage and let him go wild. I hope he would find it a tribute and that he might have found a meaning in the piece that he could endorse. And also above all that it might give him a laugh.

As I sincerely hope it does you.

Since the beginning of our collaboration, which began even before a word was written, Alan Dossor and I have been determined to create a piece uniting two worlds that are often kept apart - that of football and of the theatre, and hopefully that of their (often separate) audiences. If Brian worked to create his vision of the beautiful game we are attempting to create our own version - with the help of an amazing team. Guided of course always by Brian himself.

Stephen Lowe
Nottingham
June 2005

CREDITS/ACKNOWLEDGEMENTS:
Cathy LeSurf, David Wilson, Tim Disney, Tanya Myers, Marcus Alton, Professor Malcom Griffiths, Giles Croft, Stephanie Sirr, Esther Richardson, Peter Preston, John from the D.H. Lawrence Research Centre and especially thanks to Alan Dossor and the whole premier team! The song **Such a Man** - lyrics: Stephen Lowe, music: David Wilson.

CAST

PROLOGUE: The Heavenly Shower

General William Booth	**James Warrior**
D.H. Lawrence	**Jamie Kenna**
Lord Byron	**Ben Goddard**
Brian Clough	**Colin Tarrant**
Perfect Little Angel	**Laura Martin Simpson**

THE SPIRIT OF THE MAN

Jimmy	**Ken Bradshaw**
Gerald/Brian Clough/Robin Hood	**Colin Tarrant**
Mick/Little John/King Richard	**Dave Nicholls**
Damien/Alan a'Dale	**Ben Goddard**
Eddy/Will Scarlet/Guy of Gisbourne	**Jamie Kenna**
Adrian/Friar Tuck	**James Warrior**
Sarah/Barbara/Maid Marian	**Laura Martin Simpson**

CREATIVE TEAM

Director	**Alan Dossor**
Designer	**Jamie Vartan**
Lighting Designer	**Mark Pritchard**
Sound Designer	**Adam McCready**
Musical Director	**Ben Goddard**
Fight Director	**Terry King**
Company and Stage Manager	**Jane Eliot-Webb**
Deputy Stage Manager	**Cath Booth**
Assistant Stage Manager	**Kathryn Bainbridge Wilson**

THE COMPANY

Ken Bradshaw
Jimmy

Theatre includes: **Four Knights in Knaresborough** (Riverside Studios); **Eden End, Johnson Over Jordan, Half a Sixpence, Spring & Port Wine, Macbeth, Enjoy, Intimate Exchanges, The Cucumber Man** (West Yorkshire Playhouse); **Blue Remembered Hills, A Naughty Night To Swim In, Bedevilled** (Sheffield Crucible); **The Wizard of Oz, The Mikado, Derby Day, Dancing at Lughnasa, Talent** (Bolton Octagon); **Venice Preserv'd** (Royal Exchange); **Stags & Hens** (Oldham Coliseum); **Doctor Faustus, The Caucasian Chalk Circle** (Liverpool Everyman); **Big Night Out** (Watford Palace); **Brassed Off** (Birmingham Rep); and **Going to the Chapel** (Salisbury Playhouse).

Television includes: **Beaten, Casualty, Julius Caesar, Time Treasures, Police 2020, Reckless, Coronation Street, Children's Ward, And the Beat Goes On, This Is Personal, Blind Ambition, Where The Heart Is, Shipman, Silent Witness, The Bill, Strange** and **Courtroom**.

Ben Goddard
Lord Byron/Damien/Alan a'Dale/ Musical Director

Theatre credits include: Juan in **Murderous Instincts, Over my Shoulder,** Amiens in **As You Like It** (Regent's Park Open Air); Paris u/s Romeo in **Romeo & Juliet** (Regent's Park Open Air); Del/John in **The Beautiful Game** (Really Useful Group); Tom in **The Glass Menagerie** (Queens Theatre); Judas in **Jesus Christ Superstar** (Really Useful Group); Inigo Jollifant in **The Good Companions** (Coventry Belgrade Theatre); Horatio in **Hamlet** (Ludlow Festival); Balthazar in **Much Ado About Nothing** (Manchester Royal Exchange); Dandini in **Cinderella - The Panto with Soul** (Theatr Clwyd); Friar Francis in **Much Ado About Nothing** (Ludlow Festival); and **Kiss The Sky** (Shepherds Bush Empire).

Television credits include: **Trial & Retribution VI** (La Plante Productions), **London Bridge** (Carlton Television) and **Bugs** (Carnival Television).

As Musical Director and Music Producer: a long list of Rock shows, Actor Muso shows and large scale music projects.

Jamie Kenna
D.H. Lawrence/Eddy/Will Scarlet/ Guy of Gisbourne

Theatre credits include: Magwitch in **Great Expectations** (Channel Theatre Company); Max Miller in **The Cheekie Chappie** (The Union Theatre); Badger in **The Wind In The Willows** (Channel Theatre); Ged Murray in **Comedians** (The Union Theatre); Black in **The Wild Party** (The Union Theatre); Ernest & Terry in **Confusions** (Leatherhead Thorndike Theatre); Terry, Harry and Mr Pearce in **Confusions** (Barons Court Theatre); and Bottom in **A Midsummer Night's Dream** (Richmond Drama School).

Feature film credits include: Keith in **The Alltogether** (Establishment Films), Big Marc in **Hooligans** (Oddlot Productions); and Dave in **It's A Casual Life** (Logie Productions).

Television credits include: Pete in **55 Degrees North** (BBC); Denny Phillips in **The Bill** (Thames Talkback Television); and Jock Livingstone in **Newhaven Port** (Eview Entertainment).

Commercial/corporate credits include:

Gary in **corporate video for Youth Justice Board**, and Jake Longley in **Budweiser commercial**.

Laura Martin-Simpson
*Perfect Little Angel/Sarah/
Barbara/Maid Marian*

Laura trained at RADA.

Theatre credits include: **A Midsummer Night's Dream** (Hampton Court Palace); **Splendour** (Cockpit Theatre); **Bash** (Judi Dench Theatre - Mountview); **Paradise for Exiles** (British Embassy, Rome, Keats' House); **Life is But a Day** (British Embassy, Rome, Keats' House); and **Comedy Of Vanity** (Union Theatre, Southwark and The Underbelly, Edinburgh).

TV credits include: **Togu** (BBC3).

Film credits include: **Sophie** (Independent Films).

Radio credits include: **Williwaw** (BBC Radio) and **Stalingrad** (BBC Radio).

Dave Nicholls
Mick/Little John/King Richard

Dave has performed seasons at York Theatre Royal, Leeds Playhouse, Manchester Royal Exchange, including: **Oedipus Rex**, **Oedipus at Colonus**, and Hannah Smith's **Casket and Pravda**.

His extensive television work includes: **Queer As Folk**, **City Central**, **Cops II The 10th Kingdom**, **The Bill**, **Best**, **Cruel Earth**, **Psychos**, **Last Hurdle**, **Whizziwig**, **A Touch Of Frost**, **Heartbeat**, **Band Of Gold**, **Wycliffe**, **A Perfect State**, **The Missing Postman**, **Ivanhoe**, **Emmerdale**, **Secrets & Lies**, **Six Sides Of Coogan**, **The Governor**, **Rumble**, **Birds Of A Feather**, **The Wanderer**, **White Goods**, **My Good Friend**, **The Detectives**, **Westbeach**, **Wide Eyed and Legless**, **Oscar Charlie**, **Stan the Man**, **Hollyoaks**, **The Long Firm**, **Steel River Blues**, **New Tricks** and **Coronation Street**.

Film work includes: **Highlander**, **Secrets and Lies**, **Gangs of New York**, **Gladiator**, **Muppet Treasure Island**, **Jack And Sarah** and **Jack and the Beanstalk The Real Story**.

Colin Tarrant
Brian Clough/Gerald/Robin Hood

Colin studied English and Drama at Exeter University before joining the community theatre group Medium Fair, which was formed out of the drama department there.

Recent credits: **The Man Who** (Orange Tree Theatre); **The Glee Club** (Bush Theatre National Tour); **Serjeant Musgrave's Dance** (Oxford Stage Company National Tour); and **Jack and the Beanstalk** (Northcott, Exeter).

Other credits: **The Life & Times of Bob Scallion** (Northcott Theatre); **Neville's Island** (Theatre Royal York); **The Soldier's Song** (Theatre Royal, Stratford East); **The Daughter-in-Law** (Birmingham Rep); **The Lower Depths**, (FocoNovo); **Cymbeline/Arabian Nights** (Shared Experience); **Six Men of Dorset** (7:84 England); **The Winter's Tale**, **Henry IV Parts I & II**, **Peter Pan** (RSC); **King Lear**, **The Rivals**, **The Bending Machine**, **Never Say Rabbit in a Boat** (Victoria Theatre, Stoke); **Stags and Hens**, **No More Sitting On The Old School Bench**, **The Dice House** (Belgrade Theatre, Coventry); and **Lady Chatterley's Lover** (Phoenix Theatre, Leicester).

Television: **The Rainbow** (BBC) and Inspector Monroe in **The Bill** (ITV).

Radio: **The Glee Club**.

James Warrior
General Willam Booth/Adrian/ Friar Tuck

James has been an actor for forty years, beginning when he left the Guildhall School of Music & Drama, where he had trained, to join the ground-breaking Brighton Combination Theatre Company. There he worked with the writers David Hare, Trevor Griffiths, Howard Brenton, Tony Bicat and many more. He was a member of Richard Eyre's company at Nottingham Playhouse in the '70s appearing in most of the productions, including **Comedians** by Trevor Griffiths playing one of the comedians, Ged Murray. He was also in the London production and the television version of this classic play.

James has appeared in many television shows including David Nobbs' **Glamour Girls**, **The Fall & Rise of Reginald Perrin**, **The Sweeney**, **Dream Team**, **The Bill**, **Casualty**, **Doctors** and **Coronation Street**. He has also been in many films including **Sweeney 2**, **The Pink Panther Strikes Again** and **I Capture the Castle**.

Now living in Devon, James is also a brewer, having recently started the Warrior Brewing Company with his wife Jude.

Stephen Lowe
Playwright

Stephen Lowe has worked as an actor, director and artistic director as well as a playwright. Born in Nottingham, he graduated from Birmingham University, where he also did post-graduate research, and for four years worked as actor/writer in Alan Ayckbourn's Scarborough Theatre in the Round before Richard Eyre directed his first major award-winning play **Touched** at Nottingham Playhouse. Since then his stage work has been performed at London's Royal Court, the RSC, Stratford East and Hampstead Theatre, as well as premieres at leading repertory theatres including Birmingham Rep, Nottingham Playhouse, Sheffield Crucible, Liverpool Playhouse, and with touring companies like Joint Stock (with plays like **Ragged Trousered Philanthropists**) or his own company, Meeting Ground. He has worked with many theatre and TV/film directors and producers including Richard Eyre, Bill Gaskill, Stephen Daldry, Danny Boyle, David Leveux, Annie Casteldine, Alan Dossor, Michael Wearing, and the New Zealand Maori team that created the award-winning film **Once were Warriors**. His television work includes the BAFTA-nominated **Tell Tale Hearts**, his BBC classic adaptation of **Scarlet and Black** starring Ewan McGregor, two films directed by Alan Dossor set in Nottingham, **Ice Dance** and **Flea Bites** starring Nigel Hawthorne, and numerous episodes of **Coronation Street**. His work has been translated and performed throughout the world and twelve of his plays have been published by Methuen. He is married to the actress Tanya Myers, and has three children. He is a council member of Arts Council England (ACE) and chair of ACE-East Midlands. His latest play **The Fox**, inspired by the novella by D.H. Lawrence, will tour the region and nationally in the autumn.

For more information visit **www.stephenlowe.co.uk**

Alan Dossor
Director

Film and television includes: **Brides in the Bath** (Yorkshire TV); **A is for Acid** (Yorkshire TV); **Where The Heart Is** (United); **A Touch Of Frost** (Yorkshire TV); **The Life and Crimes of William Palmer** (YTV); **The Missing Postman** (BBC - Winner British Comedy Awards Best Drama 1997); **The Locksmith** (Fair Games Film/BBC); **No Bananas** (BBC); **The Governor** (La Plante Productions); **Between The Lines** (Island World/BBC TV); **Fair Game** (BBC); **Flea Bites** (BBC); **Broke** (BBC); **First And Last**

(BBC - Winner - International Emmy Award); **Ice Dance** (BBC); and **Star Quality** (BBC).

Alan has directed over forty dramas for television, sixteen of them films. These include the video series **Connie** starring Stephanie Beacham (Central TV), **Home Video** starring Patricia Routledge and Colin Blakeley (Limehouse/Channel 4), the film series **Johnny Jarvis** (BBC), and the highly acclaimed film **Muscle Market** with Pete Postlethwaite (BBC).

Alan has directed over fifty stage productions in the English regions, London West End, Canada and Broadway. From 1970-75 he was Artistic Director at the Everyman Theatre, Liverpool, where he directed a mixture of classics and many new plays. Among the writers were John McGrath, Adrian Mitchell, Willy Russell, Mike Stott, C. P. Taylor and Charles Wood.

Recent theatre productions include: **Spring and Port Wine**, **Single Spies**, **Enjoy** and **Intimate Exchanges** (all at West Yorkshire Playhouse).

Original and subsequent West End productions include: **John, Paul, George, Ringo and Bert** (Winner E S Best Musical), **Funny Peculiar** and **Breezeblock Park**.

London productions include: **Comings and Goings** (Hampstead); **Flying Blind** (Royal Court); **Liberty Hall** (Greenwich); **Having a Ball** (Lyric Hammersmith); **Rose** (Lyric); **Dracula** (Young Vic); and **Harvest** (Ambassadors).

Jamie Vartan
Designer

Jamie Vartan trained at Central St. Martin's School of Art & Design, London. In 1988 he was awarded an Arts Council Bursary to work at Nottingham Playhouse where he designed several productions. He also previously designed **Because It's There** and **Angels Among the Trees** at Nottingham Playhouse.

He has worked extensively at the National Theatre of Ireland (The Abbey & Peacock Theatres) including designs for two consecutive productions of **The Playboy of the Western World**, also **Blackwater Angel**, **The Hostage**, **A Little Like Paradise**, **Sour Grapes**, **Making History**, **Mrs Warren's Profession** (nomination for Irish Times Theatre Awards Best Production) and the premiere of Colm Toibin's new play **Beauty In A Broken Place**.

He was involved for three years as designer and artist-in residence with the David Glass Ensemble on **The Lost Child Trilogy**, with residencies involving workshops, research and new devised productions in Vietnam, Indonesia, China, the Philippines and Colombia. The Trilogy was later presented at the Young Vic. **The Hansel Gretel Machine** (part one of the trilogy) was selected for the 1999 Prague Quadrennial Theatre Design Exhibition.

Design for dance with choreographer Darshan Singh Bhuller includes **Recall** at the Linbury Studio (Royal Opera House and UK tour) and **Requiem** for Phoenix Dance Theatre (Sadlers Wells and UK tour).

Designs for opera include: **La Traviata** (Malmo Musikteater, Sweden); **A Village Romeo and Juliet** (L'Opera magazine nomination best set & costume design 2002) and **Aida** (Teatro Lirico di Cagliari, Sardinia); **The Dwarf** (Teatro Comunale, Florence and Teatro Regio, Turin); **La Statira** (Teatro San Carlo, Naples); **The Queen Of Spades** (La Scala, Milan); and currently **Carmen** (Cagliari); and **May Night** (Garsington Opera 2006).

Mark Pritchard
Lighting Designer

Mark has lit more than 40 productions in the West End, the first being **Mrs Wilson's Diary** at the Criterion Theatre and including **The Secret of Sherlock Holmes** at Wyndhams, **Time and the Conways** at the Old Vic, **Cotton Club** at the Aldwych, **Present Laughter** at the

Globe and The Aldwych Theatres, **Miracle Worker** at the Comedy and **In Praise of Love** at the Gielgud Theatre.

For the Royal Shakespeare Company he has designed **Romeo and Juliet** and **Hamlet**.

Opera and ballet productions include work for Sadlers Wells Royal Ballet and The Stuttgart Ballet, Phoenix Opera, Kent Opera, three seasons for Dublin Opera, a season at the Wexford Opera Festival, Handel's **Ottone** at the Q.E.H. and the World Premiere of Peter Maxwell Davies' **Martyrdom of St. Magnus** in Kirkwall Cathedral in the Orkneys.

Mark has worked extensively abroad including productions at the National Theatres of France (T.N.P.), Iceland and Ireland (The Abbey), also at the Gate Theatre in Dublin. He has lit many shows in Denmark including the world premiere of Solzhenitsyn's **Love Girl and the Innocent** (Aalborg) and the European premiere of **Sunday in the Park with George** (Copenhagen). Also in Copenhagen **Sweeney Todd**, **Candide**, **Les Miserables**, a new Danish Musical **Atlantis**, and **Miss Saigon**.

Mark has worked in most regional theatres in England lighting **Pickwick** at Chichester and on tour, **How Was it For You** and **Fair Game** at the Theatre Royal Plymouth, **The Miracle Worker** and **In Praise of Love** at the Thorndike Theatre. **The Cherry Orchard** at the Haymarket Theatre Leicester. At the West Yorkshire Playhouse he has lit **Sugar**, **The Merchant of Venice**, **Mail Order Bride**, **Call in the Night**, **Pilgerman** and **King Lear** (also at the Hackney Empire) and **The Beatification of Area Boy** by Wole Soyinka, which included a European Tour (also going to New York and The Sydney and Perth Festivals). **The Winter's Tale** and **The Fireraisers** at The Bridewell Theatre in London. **Kings** at the Tricycle Theatre. **Times Up** and **Move Over Mrs Markham** at the Theatre Royal Windsor. **Vanity Fair** and **Jar the Floor** at the West Yorkshire Playhouse. **The Turn of the Screw** at The Queen's Theatre Hornchurch and **Pygmalion** and the new musical **Stepping Out** at the Albery Theatre. **Secret Spies** (directed by Alan Dossor) at the West Yorkshire Playhouse and **Mind Game** at the Vaudeville Theatre. **Hard Times, French without Tears** and **Vanity Fair** at the Northcott Theatre, Exeter. Also **Chasing the Duchess of Malfi**, **At Home with the Cripps** and **The Monk** for Theatre Resource. **A Midsummer Night's Dream**, **Dear Brutus**, **Travels with my Aunt**, **Mary Rose**, **The Mill on the Floss** and **The Tempest** at Nottingham Playhouse.

Mark has just finished his eighth season at Pitlochry Festival Theatre and has recently lit **The People Next Door** for the Traverse Theatre Edinburgh, the Belgrade Festival in Serbia and the E.59 St. Theatre in New York. He has been a Board member of the Theatre Royal, Stratford East for 20 years. He was nominated for the 2004 Scottish Critics Theatre awards for his lighting for **Double Indemnity**.

Adam McCready
Sound Designer

Adam has been at Nottingham Playhouse since January 2004 after working at Derby Playhouse, Leicester Haymarket and touring the UK as sound operator for several musicals including **Blood Brothers, Whistle Down the Wind, Fame, Leader of the Pack,** and **Soul Train**. Adam also operated and sound designed the current West End production of **Joseph and his Amazing Technicolour Dreamcoat**. His previous sound designs for Nottingham Playhouse include the Eclipse UK tour of **Mother Courage and her Children, Sleeping Beauty** and **Chicken Soup with Barley**.

Terry King
Fight Director

Terry has worked extensively as a fight director in theatre, opera, musicals and television.

Theatre credits include: **Jerry Springer The Opera** (National Theatre and Cambridge); **His Dark Materials** (National Theatre) **The Jacobean Season** (Royal Shakespeare Company); and **Chitty Chitty Bang Bang** (Palladium). Terry has worked extensively for the RSC and most recently its production of **Henry VI Parts I, II & III**. He has worked also for the National Theatre, The Globe Theatre and the Royal Court.

His opera credits include productions for the Welsh National Opera, the English National Opera and Glyndebourne.

His musical credits include: **Martin Guerre**, **West Side Story**, **Saturday Night Fever** and **Jesus Christ Superstar**.

TV credits include: **The Bill**, **A Kind Of Innocence**, **The Widowing of Mrs Holroyd**, **Measure for Measure**, **Death of a Salesman**, **EastEnders**, **Casualty**, **Fell Tiger**, **A Fatal Inversion** and **Broken Glass**.

Previous work for Nottingham Playhouse includes **As You Like It**, **Big Night Out at the Little Sands Picture Palace**, **Neville's Island**, **Rats, Buckets and Bombs**, **Wonderful Tennessee**, **Beautiful Thing**, **Moon on a Rainbow Shawl**, **Rat Pack Confidential**, **Othello** and **Angels Among the Trees**.

Nottingham Playhouse
theatre company

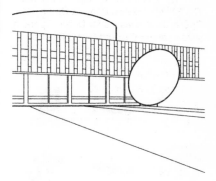

Nottingham Playhouse Theatre Company creates thirteen productions per year on all scales. From 2002-2005 the Playhouse toured its work to over fifty towns and cities in the UK and Europe. In the same period London transfers include its world premiere production of **Rat Pack Confidential**, **Mother Courage and her Children** (after a national tour), **The Railway Children** and **Little Sweet Thing** (after a national tour).
Roundabout's production of **Mohammed** featured in the Mejnifest Celebrations to mark the accession of Slovenia into the European Community in May 2004. In 2005 it co-produced with Octagon Theatre, Bolton, Birmingham Rep, The New Wolsey Ipswich, Northern Stage, Tricycle Theatre, Sadler's Wells, Coventry Belgrade, the Royal Lyceum Theatre Edinburgh and The Thalia Theater, Hamburg.

Nottingham Playhouse has a commitment to commissioning new work and has staged five world premieres on its main stage and three touring works for children in 2004/05. Nominated for a dozen awards between 2002-2005, it won the

City Life award for Best Production for
Rat Pack Confidential.

For more information on our work see
www.nottinghamplayhouse.co.uk

Stephanie Sirr
Chief Executive

Giles Croft
Artistic Director

Nottingham Playhouse's work is made
possible with the help and support of:

Rushcliffe

Arts & Business

Nottingham Playhouse is a member of:

Experience
Nottinghamshire

 Nottingham Playhouse is the
only UK member of the
European Theatre
Convention

Photo courtesy of Martine Hamilton Knight

Photo: Robert Day

**The following companies support the
work of Nottingham Playhouse
through sponsorship of major
projects, individual productions and
support in kind, or through our
corporate membership scheme,
_in_BUSINESS.**

Thanks to our business partners:

Sponsors
The Ark Day Nursery
Bentley Jennison
Childs Play Nursery
Derbyshire Building Society
De Facto
Experian
Hello Telecom
Hoofers Gym Dance & Fitness
Midland Mainline
Pennine Telecom
Presence - The Internet Specialists
Russell Scanlan Insurance
The University of Nottingham

_in_BUSINESS members
Barclays Bank Plc
Browne Jacobson
Edwards Geldard Solicitors
IBM (UK) Ltd
Orchid (UK) Ltd

_in_HOUSE Business
The Bookcase
Regent Street Dental Practice
Goodman East Midlands
Financial Services
Tomkins Florists

Lifestyle
Premier Travel Inn

We would like to thank the following companies and individuals for their kind assistance with this production:

D.H. Lawrence Research Centre, Nottingham University

Nottingham Central Library

Soundcontrol
www.soundcontrol.co.uk

Tony Rotherham of Spirit of England Medieval Theatre Company

Bowood House, Wiltshire

We gratefully acknowledge the assistance of

Persil

Comfort

Persil
Silk & Wool

courtesy of
LEVER FABERGÉ
in providing Wardrobe Care.

Nottingham Playhouse

Wellington Circus
Nottingham
NG1 5AL

Box Office 0115 941 9419

Minicom 0115 947 6100

Fax 0115 924 1484

www.nottinghamplayhouse.co.uk

enquiry@nottinghamplayhouse.co.uk

Nottingham Playhouse theatre company

Administration

Janet Clifford	Accounts Assistant
Alison Jones	Head of Finance & Administration (Maternity Cover)
Sooki McShane	Casting Director
Jill Robertshaw	Administration Officer
Jean Sands	Contracts Manager
Kurt Sickelmore	Finance Manager
Myra Slack	Wages Clerk
Rachael Thomas	Head of Finance & Administration

Cleaning and Maintenance

Kevin Bates	Cleaner
Cath Finch	Cleaner
Anne Lovewell	Head Cleaner
Sheila Sisson	Cleaner
Michael Turton	Maintenance Technician
Maureen Wheat	Cleaner
Paul White	Cleaner

Construction

Mark Bamford	Carpenter
Lex Brown	Freelance Carpenter
Conrad Cooper	Freelance Fabricator
Philip Gunn	Deputy Head of Construction
Julian Smith	Head of Construction
Steve Knight	Freelance Fabricator
Ray Wilkins	Freelance Carpenter

Directors

Richard Baron	Associate Director
Giles Croft	Artistic Director
Stephanie Sirr	Chief Executive
Brenda Frost	PA to Chief Executive & Artistic Director

Front of House

Sophie Batten-Holdway	Usher
Tim Challen	Fireman
Karen Creedy	Usher
Laura Culley	Usher
Rebecca Dallman	Theatre Manager
Alison Davey	Usher
Clare Devine	Usher
Myah Ellis	Usher
Chris Evans	Volunteer
Shirley Greenow	Usher
Caroline Hardy	Usher
Carol Harmer	Usher

Luke Harvey	Usher
Abbei Heathcote	Usher
Livia McLauchlan	House Manager
Dave Richardson	Usher
Jeanette Severn	Usher
Laura Smith	Usher
Richard Swainson	House Manager
Brendan Winslow	Usher
Stephen Woods	Usher

Lighting & Sound

Drew Baumohl	Lighting & Sound Technician
Adam McCready	Deputy Head of Lighting & Sound
Nick Morris	Lighting & Sound Technician
Paul Stear	Head of Lighting and Sound

Marketing and Development

Clare Alderson	Box Office Assistant
Stacey Arnold	Communications Officer
Rachael Bevan	Box Office Supervisor
Mark Crane	Box Office Supervisor
Anne Denman	Development Officer
Matthew Dix	Box Office Assistant
Daryll Garavan	Box Office Assistant
Derek Graham	Marketing Officer
Ed Green	Marketing Assistant
Jacqueline Hughes	Box Office Supervisor
Nadia Lane	Box Office Assistant
Emma O'Neil	Box Office Assistant
Angela Opacic	Box Office Assistant
Richard Surgay	Sales & Customer Services Manager
Sally Anne Tye	Head of Marketing & Development
Chris Wharton	Box Office Assistant
Emma Williams	Box Office Assistant

Paint & Props

Sophie Brown	Deputy Head of Paintshop
Rebecca Denning	NTU Student Placement
Sarah Richard	Head of Paintshop
Nathan Rose	Head of Props
Celia Strainge	Deputy Head of Props

Production

D Sawyerr	Production Manager
Denzil Hebditch	Assistant Production Manager

Casual Production Staff

Nick Roberts, Jacob Corn, Ben Kelly, Aurelie Rogué, Ian Downing, Gareth Chell, Mark Dawson and Marcus Birkin.

Roundabout & Education

Andrew Breakwell	Director
Kitty Parker	Administrator
Allie Spencer	Theatre Workshop Leader
Trina Haldar	Trainee Workshop Leader
Emma Rosoman	Writer in Residence
Bea Udeh	BRIT Officer

Stage Door

Vilma Bent	Stage Doorkeeper
James Broughton	Stage Doorkeeper
Geoff Linney	Stage Doorkeeper
Geoff Nightingale	Stage Doorkeeper
Garry Parsons	Stage Doorkeeper
Rosemarie Potts	Senior Receptionist
Susan Yeoman	Receptionist

Stage Management & Technical

Andy Bartlett	Technical Manager
Cath Booth	Deputy Stage Manager
Jamie Bridges	Stage Technician
Anita Drabwell	Deputy Stage Manager
Jane Eliot-Webb	Company & Stage Manager
Ryan Grant	Deputy Technical Manager
Kathryn Bainbridge Wilson	Assistant Stage Manager

Wardrobe

Heather Flinders	Wardrobe Assistant (Maintenance)
Lucy Machin	Dresser
Maggie Power	Wardrobe Assistant
Helen Tye	Head of Wardrobe
Jude Ward	Freelance Seamstress
Chrissie Weeds	Freelance Seamstress

Theatre Writing Partnership

Sarah Françoise	Theatre Writing Assistant
Esther Richardson	Theatre Writing Director

Audio Describers

Jane Edwards
Derek Graham
Livia McLauchlan
Tullia Randall
Katie Yapp

Volunteers

Nottingham Playhouse is grateful for services donated by the following volunteers: Sylvia Draycott, Margaret James, Wendy Johnson, Daisy Rudd and Liz Squires.

Old Big 'Ead

in

The Spirit of the Man

Characters

Jimmy/D.H. Lawrence
Brian/Gerald/Robin Hood
William Booth/Adrian/Friar Tuck
Lord Byron/Damien/Alan a' Dale
Mick/Little John/Richard the Lionheart
Eddy/Will Scarlet/Guy of Gisbourne
Perfect Little Angel/Maid Marian/Sarah

The play is here, now and then and maybe tomorrow.

The script of the play incorporates all of the changes that occurred during the rehearsal process. It should therefore be regarded as the definitive version.

Prologue: The Heavenly Shower

The sound of showers. Steam. As it lifts, three men are sitting on a changing-room bench.

In addition to a towel wrapped around him, the thin, consumptive **D.H. Lawrence** *sports beard, straw hat and walking stick; next, the much healthier looking* **Lord Byron**, *similarly towelled, but with a headband, cartridge belt slung over his shoulder and a curved oriental scimitar; and finally,* **William Booth** *has to content himself with towel, his general's hat, a fine beard, a collection box and a tambourine. A man is singing.*

> Robin Hood, Robin Hood,
> Riding through the glen.
> Robin Hood, Robin Hood,
> With his band of men,
> Feared by the bad, loved by the good,
> Robin Hood, Robin Hood, Robin Hood.

Booth If he sings that song again, I swear I'll swing for him.

Lawrence (*shocked*) General. Please.

The song finishes.

Booth Blessed relief. Thank you, Lord.

The echoing tannoy.

Perfect Little Angel (*in broad Scottish voice*) Mr D.H. Lawrence. Mr Lord Byron. Mr General Booth.

They all perk up.

Perfect Little Angel Nay messages.

They all perk down. Sighs all round. Silence.

Byron (*sighs*) God, I'm desperate for a revolution.

Lawrence Sexual, political or religious?

Byron The whole caboodle. Well, we could all do with an outing, could we not?

Lawrence (*eventually*)   Have you seen the new chap, George?

Byron   Not had the pleasure.

Lawrence   Anything known about him?

Byron   Not a thing.

Booth   As long as he's not another damned shower singer!

From the shower, the singing of **Robin Hood** *as* **Brian** *arrives, betowelled, a whistle around his neck, and holding a football. He carries a sports bag with his green shirt sticking out.*

Brian   Room for a little 'un?

He squeezes in between **Lawrence** *and* **Byron**.

So what's the score, young man?

Lawrence (*baffled*)   Score?

Brian   What's the game here?

Byron   They haven't told you?

Brian   No, a very nice young woman, lady, took me postal code, stamped me East Midlands Division, bade me take a shower and wait on the bench.

Booth   That would be the Perfect Little Angel.

Brian   Frankly, I thought she should have more clothes on, but nowadays –

Booth   Don't concern yourself with that. Angels are sexless.

Brian   Good thing too. Women and showers – I've struggled to keep them apart all my life.

Lawrence   I've been totally the opposite. Whenever it rained, I was out there bursting through the bracken with the darkest passion.

Brian   Who have I the honour of talking to?

Lawrence   David Herbert Lawrence. D.H.

Brian   Brian Clough. B.H.

Lawrence (*confused*)   B.H.? (*Coughs.*)

Brian   Bad cough you got there, son. You'd have thought Heaven would have cured that.

Lawrence   Heaven's not a cure, it's a condition.

Brian   I've read some of your books, young man, well, one any road, I didn't read all of it of course, just pages 350 to 373 in that bright red Penguin edition, where Lady C. makes a chain of wild flowers to go round that gamekeeper's –

Booth   If you wouldn't mind, sir.

Brian   Sorry, no wish to offend. No, actually, when you get past the mucky bits and start describing fauna and flora I think you're bloody great. I always said to the lads to take up flowers instead of fornication, it's nowhere near as sticky. I'm a sweet-peas man myself. They named one after me. Beautiful shade. Salmon orange. After my rosy cheeks. And you are, young man – ?

Byron   Lord Byron. Call me George.

Brian   You've got a nice one there, George.

Byron   The Greeks gave it to me at Missolonghi.

Brian   That's why I never went there on holiday. Much safer in Majorca.

Byron   They buried my heart under a tree there.

Brian   Nice touch. And how are you going, General Booth?

Booth   How did you guess?

Brian   Only know two blokes who go round bashing a tambourine, and Bob Dylan were still alive when I left. Now your Sally Army band were a team I admired, you were really early socialists, with God tacked on for good measure. If you'd have dropped Him, you'd have cracked it.

Booth   Yes, well, He did rather run the whole thing.

Brian   Don't believe it. Chairmen. All the same. They all reckon they're bloody God.

Booth   He is God.

Brian   Not when it comes to football, young man.

Byron   Is that your particular area of expertise?

Brian   You've got it in one, Georgie.

Lawrence   And is football inspiring?

Brian   Does it need to be?

Lawrence   Well, that's the whole point. That's why we are all here.

Brian   Lost me.

Byron   We are the male section of the East Midlands Inspirational Spirits Division.

Brian   What's that when it's at home?

Lawrence   We are on call to inspire the living in our particular area of concern. I do sex and art.

Byron   Sex and politics.

Booth   No sex and religion.

Brian   And who was the man with the big quiver in the shower?

Booth   That would be Robin Hood. He doesn't go out much nowadays.

Byron   In his time, he was a real inspiration but . . . well, he's rather past his peak now. He occasionally pops out for the children.

Brian   And what does he cover?

Lawrence   No sex but plenty of fresh air.

Byron   So we were pondering how you might fit on the team.

Brian   Self-evident, sunshine. Football covers all you lot and a bit more. So, how long do we sit here waiting for the call?

Booth   Depends. Can be some considerable time.

Brian   Not for me, sunshine. English football has disappeared up its own back passage. Ever since that spineless bunch of England selectors turned me down for the manager's job. I waited all my life for their call, but it'll come now – and better late than never!

Lawrence   Don't be too sure. When feminism was in full swing nobody called me for twenty years.

Byron   And I haven't had a really decent revolution since Cuba.

Booth   I was called out recently in the American Mid-west, but it was really a wrong number.

Brian   No, no, different with me. You see, no offence, but men can go a fair time without sex, politics or religion, but they can hardly get through the month of August without a game of footie. Any minute now.

Byron   (*eventually*)   Do you wrestle?

Brian   Only with wine corks.

Byron   What about you, Lorenzo?

Lawrence   I once wrote a rather legendary chapter with two men nude-wrestling. All a question of Will, you know. The Life Will versus the Death. Of course, it had to be nude. It needed that mythic, classical dimension.

Byron   Classical? Very good. Well, come on, I'm bored rigid here. Let's try and bring art into life. Or whatever state we are in here.

As they disappear into the mist the **Perfect Little Angel** *enters, on roller skates. She's a little confused.*

Booth   Anything for me, my Perfect Little Angel?

Perfect Little Angel (*in thick Scottish accent*)   Oh, I've no got a clue. (*Holding up a piece of paper.*) I shouldn't be here, I'm Glasgow South be rights, but they just keep shunting us around every time them selected for the choir need to perform. I'm flying about all over the place.

Brian   So where are your wings?

Perfect Little Angel   You try getting through them flap doors wearing a six-foot pair of wings. They're only good for Sunday best. And look at this, would you? (*Holding out the paper.*) I beg them dinna write the message in ink, soon as it hits the steam in here it runs away with itself . . . now what does it say now? – something to do with . . . I can no make out anything . . . just the one wee word 'forest'. And 'lost'. Is that despair? Obviously some wee sod in a terrible state. All I can make out are the words 'lost' and 'forest'.

Brian   It's for me, young woman! Not surprised. My old team. I took them to the heights, more cups than the Queen's tea party, and then . . . well, I blew it, to be truthful, lost me bottle – no, truth was I didn't lose it, would have been better if I had –

Booth   I've always been against the bottle.

Brian   Easier said than done in my line. Any road, I left the poor little buggers in the proverbial, and they've been wallowing there ever since. Payback time, I took them from nowhere to the top, I'll bloody well do it again. So come on, beam me down, Scotty.

Perfect Little Angel (*as she presses the lift button*)   Have you any idea how many times I've heard that?

Brian (*as she goes*)   Sorry, my young angel.

Booth (*rising*)   Might as well go and rehearse the choir. Just in case.

Brian   That was always your problem, wasn't it?

Booth   What?

Brian   You never had any decent songs.

Booth (*sighs*)   Aye, well, the Devil had stolen the best tunes.

Brian   Ye', and he gave them all to Frank Sinatra. Bless him.

*As **Booth** disappears into the mist and **Brian** waits, he begins to sing his version of Sinatra's 'I Did It My Way', comprising a mixture of the following lines and verses from the original.*

And now, the lift is near,
And I have faced the final curtain.
My friends, I'll say it clear,
I'll state my case of which I'm certain . . .

Regrets, I've had a few,
I should have had the number-one job
I did what I had to do,
Was only blocked by some London snob.

I managed each and every game –
Each careful shot along the byway,
And more much more than this,
I did it my way!

For what's a manager to do
As he paces on the touchline
But shout a thing or two he feels
And not the words of one who kneels.
Let the record show I took the blows but –

They did it MY WAY!

*On the chorus the lift doors slide open, to reveal that it is full of football trophies and Forest scarves and memorabilia. **Brian** enters and sings the chorus.*

Lift   Going down.

As the doors close, the mist spreads. The sound of the ring of a mobile phone. It's ring tone is 'My Way'.

Act One

Scene One: Babes in the Wood

Sherwood Forest. Mist. The Major Oak — a giant hollow tree (the original has a girth of ten metres and span of twenty-eight) — which will also transform into a magic portal/fifties café/Majorcan bar, etc. The bench remains. **Jimmy** *stands, desperately going through all his pockets for his mobile.*

Jimmy *is a middle-aged man who finds it difficult to finish sentences at the best of times, or he launches into a torrent only realising where he was heading when he gets to the end — and even then only sometimes. He prefers to have time and seclusion to compose his dialogues. Right now he is morose, furious, wet and totally out of* joie de vivre.

Jimmy   Where . . . Where . . . Oh, God, I hate that bloody tune, she knows how much I hate it, why did I let her do this to me? (*Finally finds the phone; answers.*) What? (*Furious.*) What? Where am I? What do you care, what do you think? — I'm on the train, darling, home soon . . . Make sure the champagne's nice and chilled . . . I don't know where the hell I am, no, not true, I do, that's exactly where I am. Hell. Look. (*He scans the place.*) Can you see, sweetie, ye', it's dark, right, well spotted, Hell's dark, not a lot of sunbathing, not Majorca in May, no, did you imagine it was? So there's me — Hell freezing over, your turn, can I have a nice picture of you all tucked up in our bed, snug as a bug in a rug, champers at the ready, G-strings a go-go. No, no, don't show me, I can see it, well, course I can, I have already, haven't I, the picture's stapled to the front of my head, you and . . . I just want to say, you cow, you bitch, don't you ever dare phone me again, how you even have the nerve now to . . . after . . . I don't want to talk to you ever . . . ever eternity plus anything. (*Wild.*) How dare you hang up on me? She hung up on me! How . . . God help me.

Threatens to kick the tree down in his rage. The phone rings again. Furious:

You bitch! After all, how . . . you . . . I can't . . . bitch! What am I doing? Where the bloody hell am I? Will somebody help me please!

A ting as the lift lands, and opens as the cragged opening of the Major Oak. **Brian**, *now in tracksuit and traditional top, steps out.*

Brian   You called, young man?

Jimmy *screams in shock.*

Brian   Sorry, son, didn't mean to make you jump out your skin. Have you clocked who I am? Speak up. Eh, you're not one of them foreigners they keep shipping in, are you? Bloody bonkers. Half the Premier League spend more time chatting the birds up at Berlitz than they do out on the pitch. Speakie the English?

Jimmy   What, er, yes, well . . .

Brian   That's a blessing, cos all I can say is corkscrew in Spanish. So where you hiding the lads, then?

Jimmy   Sorry?

Brian   You've not got the poor buggers doing cross-country, packs on the back and all that bollocks? Jack that in, son, straight away. The only thing they need on their backs is the right number. And that's your job. I've known great players who'd need a bus to run 'em from one end of the pitch to t'other, but they could nod any ball into the back of the net while puffing on a Player's Full Strength. There's just three rules your lads need: make sure the buggers are shaved, showered and no shagging on match days. After that, let them do what the hell they like. Would you stop looking at me like I'm dead?

Jimmy   But sorry, you are . . . you are dead.

Brian   Don't rub me face in it, sunshine. I'm here to try to help you.

Jimmy   Sorry . . . to do what exactly?

Brian   Get your team back up to Premier, and pick up a few trophies en route.

Jimmy Yes. (*Quietly.*) Yes. Yes. Just a . . . would you mind, I'm having a terrible . . . I'm just, I'm just going to close my eyes for a few seconds and then . . . you know, so thank you very much and goodbye. (*Closes his eyes, opens them.* **Brian** *is still there. Restrained.*) Okay, you're not going to go away are you? Right, okay, that's fine, hallucination, okay, fine, at least you're not a giant rabbit called Harvey . . . given that you are my hallucination, that's fine, that's not a problem, but I'm confused that . . . that you're confused . . . because mad as this is at the same time even madness is supposed to have its own logic and –

Brian Spit it out, son.

Jimmy You seem to imagine I'm some sort of football manager.

Brian Aye, some sort is about right. And I'm here to inspire you and your lads.

Jimmy Yes, well, thank you very much, I mean that's exceedingly . . . very . . . but you see I'm not. I'm not a football manager.

Pause.

Brian But you want to be?

Jimmy Not especially, no.

Brian I don't believe that, I mean every man –

Jimmy Not me, no, sorry. Don't mean to offend you.

Brian So what the hell are you?

Jimmy I'm a playwright. I write plays.

Brian (*a beat*) Like Ernie Wise?

Jimmy To be honest, I'm not that good.

Brian Well, I'll go to the foot of our stairs. So what were you doing asking for help wi' Forest? They said you'd lost again?

Jimmy   Well, er, I am lost certainly. In the forest.

Brian   Bloody hell. A right balls up that is. If I ran Heaven like – never mind . . . writer you say?

Jimmy   On a good day, but this –

Brian   They've sent you the wrong bloke. Not being personal, but what you like with sex?

Jimmy   Well, not very good.

Brian   You need that D.H. bloke to come and have a chat with you. Don't worry. I'll sort it out. All the best to you, young man.

Jimmy   Ye', thank you, well, nice to have . . .

Brian   (*goes to the tree*)   Beam me up, Scotty.

He disappears into the tree.

Jimmy   Right, okay . . . steady. Calm down. People . . . it's not usual . . . people see things . . . pink elephants . . . least he's not a pink elephant . . . the mind plays . . . No, no more drink obviously, Jimmy. But we haven't had a drink. Perhaps we should. Not the point. What is the point? You're talking to yourself. Who, who's talking? Listen to me. What? You're right, this is perfectly understandable, there's a perfectly rational explanation to all this. Oh, good. Good. Yes, the truth is you've been barking for years, and somehow managed to get away with it and even sometimes get paid for it. But you know, face it . . . day of reckoning . . . reckoning . . . all the chickens and the cockerels home to roost . . . roosters. Home. Yes. In my home, the cockerel is in my own home. Right now. Roostering or what the bloody word is with – (*Furious.*) Steady, steady. (*Deep breaths.*)

Brian   (*reappears*)   Lifts. They take an eternity, don't they?

Jimmy   (*politely*)   Yes, don't they just?

Brian   (*as he disappears*)   Come on, my Perfect Little Angel.

Jimmy   It's going to be okay. Steady. Just hold on in. Day will dawn and there'll be a bright golden haze on the . . . it's not *King Lear*. Not the blasted heath. Be fine.

Brian   (*reappearing*)   Sorry to bother you, sunshine.

Jimmy   (*holding on by a thread*)   Ah. No problem.

Brian   It's just the lift's not working.

Jimmy   I'm afraid I'm not very mechanical. I did art at school instead of –

Brian   No, that's not what I meant, young man. Something odd here. You sure you're not interested in football?

Jimmy   Positive.

Brian   Bloody funny is that. So what are you interested in?

Jimmy   Nothing.

Brian   Nothing?

Jimmy   That's right. Absolutely nothing. You see, Mr Clough, I'm going to talk as though, you see, right now I am actually in the middle of a major existentialist nightmare. If there was something then it wouldn't be, but there isn't. Only nothing.

Brian   You're a bit down in the dumps, then? What's got your goat?

Jimmy   Oh, well, let me see, where should we begin? Well, yes, my work. My work, haven't been able to write anything for months. I've a theatre waiting for a script breathing down my neck every five minutes, I promised them a play with local interest, local interest, I don't have any local interests . . . because my particular inspiration, my love . . . I *knew* there was something wrong . . . I knew, I knew . . . then today . . . I arrive home unexpected, to find my wife with our gardener. He was doing what looked to be a very proficient job bedding her in. In our bed. We pay him by the hour. I don't know whether this was something he was doing in his own time. He seemed an honest enough guy.

Brian   So what did you do, son, did you kill them both?

Jimmy   Yes, of course. Immediately. As you do in films. Of course. No. No. No.

Brian   Did you at least chuck a bucket of water over them?

Jimmy   Amazingly that didn't occur to me. No. I just . . . I just waved and – (*gestures*) just a little wave to let them know . . . He couldn't see me but . . . she . . .

Brian   What did she say?

Jimmy   Well, at that precise moment, it was rather difficult for her to say . . . not that if she could have spoke . . . I really prefer not to talk about this if you don't mind.

Brian   I just want to know what you did.

Jimmy   I walked.

Brian   Walked?

Jimmy   Yes.

Brian   To anywhere in particular?

Jimmy   There is no destination in existentialism.

Brian   Makes booking your holidays pretty tough. Sorry, I'm not tekin' the piss. That's bloody awful. (*Eventually.*) I'm not very good with these emotional things. I tend to leave feelings to the wife. Well, you do, don't you? Well, *you* don't, shouldn't, but . . . Sorry. (*To himself.*) Foot on the ball, Brian. Slow the game down a bit. (*Pause.*) So, what's your name, son?

Jimmy   Jimmy.

Brian   Listen, Jimmy, by the looks of it I can't get back for a shower until I've inspired you. Probably nobody up there's willing to admit to a cock-up, in my experience them on high never do, so I don't know, there must be some way I can get your juices flowing. You write plays, right?

Jimmy   Yes.

Brian   Bet they're full of four-letter words, aren't they?

Jimmy   Usually.

Brian   I hate that. You switch on the telly and there's always some bugger effing and blinding.

Jimmy   That's probably one of mine.

Brian   Ernie Wise never had truck with swearing.

Jimmy   He's a role model to us all. I'm going to wake up in a minute and everything's going to be okay.

Brian   What do you write about?

Jimmy   Nothing.

Brian   You're right. I've seen a lot of your stuff. Come on, they must be about something?

Jimmy   I fooled myself they were, but I know now it's not true.

Brian   But you must believe in something?

Jimmy   I did once. Too many things.

Brian   Like what?

Jimmy   Like you.

Brian   What?

Jimmy   There were a photo of you in the *Evening Post*. You leading a support march for the miners' strike, 1984. I kept that picture, not for you, but for the elbow in the corner. That was me − duffle coat, wooden woggles, burdened with badges. I believed in everything then. I don't know, pyramids, ley lines, communication with the dead. God, I even believed British telly would get better, and that truth would always triumph, and then Thatcher beat the miners and made it rain all the time, every bloody day for a generation, and . . . (*Singing bitterly.*)

I believed
For every drop of rain that falls
A flower grows . . .

Brian Did I touch a little button there, son? (*Pause.*) Tragic is that.

Jimmy Would you go away, please, and leave me be.

Brian No, no, it's the only word for it, tragic, I mean, you spend all that money buying badges and then it rains so you can't go out to play? Listen to me, young man, life isn't cricket. Any halfwit knows that. It's footie. The whole point of football is, you play at the worst time of year when it's pissing down, and you have to slog it out up to your crown jewels in muck and bullets. I'm not saying it's trench warfare but it's bloody close. And of course you get slammed down now and again. When I were twenty-six I were the highest goal-scorer over two seasons – at the top of my game. Out on that pitch all I could see were two posts, a crossbar and a net, and in front of it some bloody ghost I were going to kick the ball right through. That ball loved me. It would search me out, like some lost babbie come home to Daddy. And it'd bounce up and stick to my foot until I'd kick the little bugger right into the back of the net. Then one freezing Boxing Day, against Bury, ice on the pitch, no underfloor heating in them days, and that bloody ghost in the goal – nice bloke, Chris Harker – slid towards me, and he just kept on sliding, couldn't do nothing about it, and he flipped me, and next thing I know I'm in a world of women in white. Didn't look like the normal dressing room to me. Cruciate ligament buggered. But I didn't give up the game. Even when it seemed to have given me up. I trained on crutches, I trained running up and down a freezing bloody beach for a season, and I clawed my way back, but not good enough. I couldn't play my part in the beautiful game, not as a striker at any rate. But as a dreamer, my friend, as a dreamer – that's what a manager is, son. A man who's got to bring his dreams into being or go mad. In't that the same for you?

Jimmy What's the point?

Brian That is the point, son. Is that exitsensualist enough for you? I'm not quite as daft as I look, am I?

Jimmy (*pauses*)   No.

Brian   So give me a chance, eh? Let's see if we can find a subject that will inspire you and I can clear off. Right, now what would Ernie Wise do? Let's take a leaf out of his book, shall we? Always turn to the best.

Jimmy (*exhausted*)   Do you mind if I sit down?

Brian   On the bench, son. I'll walk the touchline. Now Ernie always picked heroes, that's what folk are into. Larger-than-life men who make their own destiny, come from nowhere, and win through no matter what life can throw at them. And you want a local interest. Now who would fit that bill – some legend in his own time, who could guarantee thirty thousand for a Saturday matinée?

Jimmy   No.

Brian   No what?

Jimmy   I'm not doing a play about Brian Clough.

Brian   Who were suggesting that? Mind you, now you say it – I'd have to think about it. I woun't want that warts-and-all biog stuff, though all the warts I have are on my face for the world to see, but . . . well, if you thought it would inspire others, you might talk me round. Casting's tricky. What about De Niro? He could learn the accent, given time.

Jimmy   I'm not doing a play about you. You've written your autobiographies, there's documentaries, biogs, DVDs of your greatest hits, buy the T-shirt. What's new to say? Besides, I hate football, and most of all I hate the thought of football on stage – pointless shower scenes, folk explaining the offside rule and still nobody understands it, three actors waving some sodding scarf in the air, and most of all, worst of all, slow-motion football like some wankers' ballet in shorts. (*Pause.*) Sorry. I hope I didn't offend . . .

Brian (*pauses*)   Just can't help some folk. Fine. Sod you. (*Turning back to the tree.*) Stone me. Staring me in the face. You know where you are, son?

Jimmy   Nowhere.

Brian   Don't start all that again. I brought me little
grandkids here. The Major Oak. Robin Hood's bar and
bistro. It was Robin Hood you were calling up. But he
couldn't hear you, he was in the shower. Robin Hood, the
most famous man of the Midlands, after me.

> Robin Hood, Robin Hood,
> Riding through the glen,
> Robin Hood, Robin Hood,
> With his band of men . . .

Used to be my signature tune at Forest. Come on, think
about it, Robin Hood.

Jimmy   Everybody's done him – Errol Flynn, Kevin
Costner, Walt Disney, even Mel Brooks in tights. I've
nothing new to say about him either. No, thank you, but for
me . . . *the rest is silence.*

Brian   Oh, come on. Give it a shot. Now Robin Hood,
what do you know about him?

Jimmy   I . . . er . . . the legend says he was the young
Earl of Huntington, but when good King Richard was off on
the Crusade his nasty brother John with the Sheriff of
Nottingham dispossessed him of his land so he had to take to
the forest.

Brian   Well, that's crap for a start. You don't want some
toffee-nosed lookalike for Prince William falling on hard
times. No, no, he was just an ordinary bloke, a good
Yorkshire lad like me –

Jimmy   He didn't come from Yorkshire.

Brian   I'm not arguing, but it were a big forest. And
maybe he was one of them jouster blokes, but he was too
good, like Paul Newman in *The Hustler*, so the JA –

Jimmy   JA?

Brian   Jousting Association, snotty bastards, so scared stiff
he'd take over the English team and get all the glory

whapping the world that they knobbled him, so-called accidental arrow in his left leg, cruciate ligament, so it slowed him down, couldn't play top game, so he takes to the woods, and then he meets up with a lass, doesn't he, some bonny young wench with sizzling dumplings –

Jimmy   Maid Marian was a lady.

Brian   Oh, ye'.

Jimmy   Am I writing this or you?

Brian   I'm just trying to get the feel of it for you, young man. So he starts robbing the rich to give to the poor, right?

Jimmy   Legend has –

Brian   Socialist. Good lad.

Jimmy   They didn't have socialism then.

Brian   Come on – redistribution of wealth? He was doing it before they invented the word. So how did he manage to rob the rich?

Jimmy   Tell me!

Brian   He gathered together a whole bunch of waifs and strays, flotsam and bloody jetsam, them that nobody wanted, like my Forest team in '78, and –

Jimmy   And what?

Brian   What did he do? He turned them into the merriest bloody band in the land.

Jimmy   So they weren't merry before?

Brian   Course they weren't. They were absolutely bloody miserable, flea-infested, homeless, pox-ridden, playing for crap teams in the wrong position, sick to the rafters with a diet of nettle soup and roll-ups. And what made them merry?

Jimmy   Was it the sacred mushroom? Or putting on funny hats and singing 'YMCA' under the greenwood tree?

Brian It was me. (*Pause.*) I mean, Robin Hood. The great team leader. He gave them a dream. Told them it was theirs for the taking. He put a bloody great grin on their faces.

Jimmy *stares at him. The distant sound of laughter.*

Brian Listen to them, laughing merrily. Oh, come on, son, start imagining. You've nothing to lose but your exitsensualism.

Silence. **Jimmy** *approaches the oak. He listens to it.*

Brian Can you hear?

Jimmy Something. But I can't see.

Brain You can, son. Believe me! Come on, do what you do. Imagine!

Light change. The laughter rises to a crescendo, before the first of the **Merrie Men** *tumbles out, giggling hysterically. It's* **Little John**, *who carries a stave and sports a Forest shirt.*

Jimmy Stop. Stop! Don't move! Don't you dare move!

Little John *freezes mid-convulsion. Suddenly, silence.*

Brian What's up? Not merry enough for you?

Jimmy It's just . . . (*Trying to remain calm.*) Granted that I'm as barking mad as a rabid wolf, but nevertheless I would just like to clarify one thing within this context of obviously complete and utter insanity. *I, me, it's me, I* am imagining this, that right?

Brian Spot on.

Jimmy And *you* are not? Even given that you are, probably, just another manifestation of my deranged mental status . . . you are not actually in any way shaping what I am imagining?

Brian Word of honour. It's all yours, young man.

Jimmy Brilliant. So perhaps you can explain . . . you see, I'm not an expert on medieval history, but I am fairly confident that the Merrie Men did not wear Notts Forest football shirts.

Pause.

Brian   Back to the dressing room, young man, and don't show your face until you're properly kitted out. (**Little John** *leaves.*) Sorry about that, sunshine.

Jimmy   Thank you.

And the others appear – **Friar Tuck**, **Will Scarlet**, *the minstrel* **Alan a' Dale** *– tumbling out in hysterics. A lot of pushing and jokey male prodding – if they were in the shower they'd be flicking towels.* **Jimmy** *puts up his hand again. They freeze.*

Jimmy   Sorry. I know they are the Merrie Men, but do they have to keep laughing all the time?

Brian   The key to a winning team. Looks like Robin Hood had the same philosophy as our Peter.

Jimmy   Peter who?

Brian   Peter Taylor. My number two. We were the Morcambe and Wise of football. Night before a game, I used to set Peter on the lads with his one-liners. He could make you piss your pants. Some managers reckon you need to wind your team up to screaming pitch for a match. Bollocks. Get 'em relaxed, laughing together, then they'll go kill for sheer pleasure.

Jimmy   But what are they laughing at?

Brian   Jokes.

Jimmy   Yes, but we haven't heard any.

Brian   Well, whose fault's that? You're the writer. It's your show.

Jimmy   But I don't know any medieval jokes. I don't even know any modern ones.

Little John *reappears in suitable attire.*

Brian (*looking into the tree*)   Is this the lot, then? This all we can have?

Jimmy   There's no money in theatre nowadays for big casts. No point imagining any more.

Brian   Can hardly scratch up a five-a-side. I'll have to make up the number. So what do you want them to do?

Jimmy   I don't . . . well, they'll storm Nottingham castle, I suppose. Prince John, he could be there to pick up the gold the Sheriff has taxed the people for, supposedly to pay the ransom for King Richard, whilst really –

Brian   Don't load them down with too much baggage, son. Just tell them which way they're kicking and blow the whistle.

He raises his arm. Distant sound of Robin's horn. As the **Merrie Men** *re-animate.*

Little John   What's going on?

Jimmy (*startled*)   Sorry.

Little John   Why have you called us? Why have you sounded Robin's horn?

Jimmy   Oh, wasn't me. It was him.

Brian   Right then lads, fall in. Know what the secret of a great team is, I'll tell you. The spine. Get the spine of the team right and everything will fall into place. (*As he checks out the troops.*) Forget all that 4–4–2, or Christmas tree bloody crap – put the big fellow here covering your back end, most important, you don't want anything banging in there, do you, and then this centre half thug in the middle, and he's set to deliver up to the man with the nice bald topper who's going to do the final head-butting, and you got two on the wings to support. Head to arse, and two arms. One man, one mind. Everybody knows their own place, and everybody knows the common goal. Bloody hell! This lot smell like porky pigs on heat!

Jimmy   They do live in a forest.

Brian   No excuse. Robin would have kept his men so sweet and sharp you could eat your spare ribs off Friar Tuck's arse. If you had a mind. Right then, young men, I don't know what you know about the Sheriff of Nottingham and his miserable men, most of whom have played at some time or other for Leeds under Don Revie –

Jimmy   No modern references, please.

Brian   Don't believe what you read in the press –

Jimmy   Hear in ballads.

Brian   – ballads! Ballads written –

Jimmy   Sung.

Brian   – sung about them, they're beatable, but don't go underestimating the buggers. And I know there's extra pressure, it being we're playing Wembley –

Jimmy   Attacking Nottingham Castle –

Brian   – Castle, and it can make you a bit edgy. Granted. And it don't help that every last lanky lout of Revie's –

Jimmy   The Sheriff's –

Brian   – mob are dirty, dirty bastards. They'll be tackling your tackle as soon as you get on pitch. Guard your gonads, but don't let them goad you. I see any of you lads play any dirty games – shirt-pulling, garroting, elbow in the face, disembowelling, anything like that – and I'll have you off in a flash and you'll be sitting on the bench –

Jimmy   In the stocks –

Brian   In the stocks? In the stocks for the rest of the season, I want to see you run straight through them –

Jimmy   With your swords –

Brian   (*sharply*)   Yes, run straight through them with your swords, as clean as a whistle and go straight for the goal.

Jimmy   The gold.

Brian   Yes. (*Irritated.*) The gold! Yes, all right.

Jimmy   Sorry, but I am the writer.

Brian   Yes, but I'm your bleedin' inspiration, give me a chance, will you?

Jimmy   It's just it sounds more and more like an Ernie Wise show.

Brian   Let me ask a question, young man. Of the two of you, you and Ernie, who is the most successful playwright?

Jimmy   Thank you.

Brian   I'm sorry, I don't mean to hurt you, son, I'm struggling here trying to make you successful. All right, just give me a bit of rope, if I slip into football mode you can iron that out later. Just let me get in the swing.

Jimmy   Okay.

Brian   So let's give the boys a run-out. Right, lads, this is it. We're going straight for the gold.

Will Scarlet (*mumbling*)   How we going to play it, gaffer?

Brian   Well, Stu, we've got a lot sick. No reserves. Basic five-a-side. Keep the ball on the ground. And remember this, young men, I want to see a beautiful game there. No need for heavy marking, but keep an eye on the big bastard Guy of Gisbourne. All set?

Alan a' Dale   Gaff, can we have a shag first?

Brian   No, you can't. And you're not taking that sheep on the bus with you.

Jimmy   You can't say that.

Brian   They don't have a bus?

Jimmy   Sheep-shagging!

Brian   That's the most truthful line we got. Come on, think about it. All them lonely men in the woods. But all right . . . your show.

Jimmy   Can we just get them fighting?

Brian   Right, lads, kick off. Let's go.

Suddenly they all move into life, swords and staves flashing through the air, as **Brian** *runs up and down by the side of them exhorting them on.*

Brian   Come on, you daft wankers, which way are you going? Come on, the bloody goal's that way. Footwork, footwork, pass, pass, cut through, slice down the middle, come on, you're a team of daft boggers, cover for him, there's three on him, help him, get up, who's got the ball, eye on the ball. All right, calm down, you're letting them run away with you. Eh you, put your foot on it, you gormless prat, call yourself a man of God, put your foot on it, bogger the praying, let's see some thinking here, you've time.

And **Friar Tuck** *puts his foot on the imaginary ball, throws away his stave and looks around, as the others slow to a halt taking him in.*

Brian   Keep the bleedin' ball on the ground.

And then, in slow motion, he makes a passing shot, as the others move almost balletically into slow-motion action, all together watching the journey of the ball. Finally it's headed in the air back again to **Friar Tuck**, *who is about to leap into the air when –*

Jimmy   Stop! Stop!

And all the players crash to the ground. **Jimmy** *is so furious, he can't speak.*

Brian   What's you up with you, young man? It was almost in the net.

Jimmy   No slow-motion football. That's what I said. That was an absolute given. Robin Hood did not invent football.

Brian   Could have done.

Jimmy   But he didn't.

Brian   How do you know?

Jimmy Everybody knows.

Brian Just ask yourself this, sunshine, how come in the entire world the first professional football team ever was Notts County? The secret of the game could have been passed down father to son for generations.

Jimmy I'm delirious. It could be malaria. You get mosquitoes in forests. I'd better sit down. (*Sits.*) This is not going to work. Even in madness, it doesn't . . .

Brian Jesus Christ, you take some inspiring, you do. Right. Give me one last throw.

Jimmy What's this one?

Brian The oldest trick in the book, sunshine. Hidden treasure.

Sudden change in lighting. The **Merrie Men** *are on their feet and fighting fit. The cries and clashes of steel ring around them.* **Brian** *suddenly attired as* **Robin Hood**.

Brian (*crying out*) This is it, brothers! This is the ultimate moment in a man's life! Forget all the old scores settled, forget all the winnings, the gold medals and trophies! This is the day that Robin came to life. When Robin met his inspiration. The day my world turns upside down. Batter the doors down, young men. Bring them down.

Explosion. The sound of a door splintering off its hinges and crashing to the floor. Smoke everywhere. **Robin** *has lost his hat and cape.*

Brian (*as Michael Caine*) You were only supposed to blow the bloody doors off!

But out of the mist comes a beautiful young woman, dressed in a fifties jiving outfit. The click and whirr of an old jukebox behind her, in a typical fifties café. **Jimmy** *is mystified.*

Jimmy What is this?

Brian Maid Marian, son. Maid Marian.

Maid Marian (*in Middlesborough accent*) Are you asking me?

Brian (*nervous*)   Ye'. I think so. If you fancy a –

Maid Marian   I do.

Brian   I'm not very good on my feet. Well, not . . .

Maid Marian   What's your name?

Brian   Brian.

Maid Marian   Barbara. Both beginning with B.

Brian   Ye'. Fantastic.

Silence. Cliff Richard on the jukebox, singing 'Living Doll'. And the two begin a slow jive, and do it very well, until the last whirl when she disappears again into the mist. And the doors clang to behind her, ringing through the forest. The stage is now empty, except for **Jimmy** *and* **Brian**.

Brian (*quietly*)   Sorry. Got a bit carried . . . sorry.

Jimmy   So even ghosts have eternal longings?

Brian   Nothing but, young man. Nothing but. (*Pause.*) But it's your show. And you need your Maid Marian to inspire you. You've got to spot her talent, and then to do ought and everything to make sure she'll be playing on your pitch.

Jimmy   Pitch.

Brian   Reheasal room. Whatever you call it. Just make sure she's playing on your side.

He flings open the 'door' in the tree, disappearing behind it as he does so. Lights change.

Scene Two: Rehearsal Room

Stage management pour through the door with rehearsal tables, chairs, scripts, odd bits of costumes, swords, staves, props of various kinds. As they disappear, a sudden silence. **Jimmy** *turns as the 'door' magically opens and a nervous young girl,* **Sarah**, *stands in the doorway. She wears jeans and a leather jacket.*

Sarah Am I the first?

Jimmy Someone has to be. Traditionally. (*Silence.*) And you've settled digs and . . . ?

Sarah Fine.

Jimmy Nervous?

Sarah Well . . .

Jimmy Not as much as I am.

Sarah You?

Jimmy I hate read-throughs. Feel so exposed. What if people just think it's funny?

Sarah Some of it is.

Jimmy Yes, but what if they laugh at the unfunny bits, or indeed don't laugh at the . . . ?

Sarah Funny bits?

Jimmy Yes.

Sarah What do you fear?

Jimmy I don't know. (*Pause.*) To be exposed as silly, I suppose.

Sarah But you are a very serious writer.

Jimmy One can be very serious and very silly at the same time.

A beat. She looks at the pile of scripts he is holding close to his chest. Behind them, unseen, **Eddy** (**Will Scarlet**) *appears and stands watching. He's in his thirties, and one of the hard-man acting school. In fact, in his bag he carries a set of weights to keep up his training, and he practises with them at the slightest opportunity.*

Sarah Is that the, er . . .

Jimmy Rewrites. I change everything all the time, constant flux, it drives some actors . . . but to me in theatre nothing's fixed, that's the whole point, isn't it, it's live, we can keep living and developing, travelling on the road even if, perhaps *especially* if, we don't know exactly where we are going . . .

Sarah   So is there no destination?

Jimmy   I think . . . there may be, but we simply don't know it.

Sarah   A question of trust?

Jimmy   Yes.

She nods. She reaches out, he hands her a script. She quietly sits down to read it. Both men watch her for a moment. **Jimmy** *hasn't noticed* **Eddy**.

Eddy   All up for grabs, then, maestro?

Jimmy (*startled*)   What is?

Eddy   The script.

Jimmy   Oh, well, not exactly grabs, Eddy.

Eddy   But we can talk about, improvise and . . . like the ending –

Jimmy   We'll work together to find it.

Eddy   That's great. Honest, it's really . . .

Jimmy   Great.

He hands him a script. **Eddy** *moves to sit near to* **Sarah**. *A rotund and nervous man* (**Adrian** – **Friar Tuck**) *enters with the tallest actor in the country* (**Mick** – **Little John**).

Jimmy   Adrian. (*Quietly.*) How are you? You going to be all right?

Adrian   Trust me, Jimmy, cross my heart, one-hundred-per-cent proof. I give you my solemn oath. I've even learnt all my lines.

Jimmy (*hands him the rewrites*)   Nothing's written in stone, Adrian.

Adrian No, but . . . it gives me confidence, you know.

Jimmy (*a beat, he nods*) Mick. How many now?

Mick Six. And another in the oven.

Adrian The man's a rabbit. Good job he's working away, give his poor little missus a rest. She'll be glad to get back on her feet.

Jimmy You're fixed up here?

Mick Staying with me sister. Great to be back in me home town.

Jimmy Where's Gerald?

Mick Just parking the Jag where everyone can see it.

Adrian At least you got a lift up from town with him.

Mick Ye', sitting on newspaper.

Gerald *enters – he is remarkable casting not only for the part of* **Robin Hood** *but also indeed for* **Brian Clough**. *As* **Jimmy** *hands out scripts –*

Gerald I only wish I'd used a broadsheet. You don't get the same coverage with a tabloid. Especially not for an arse his size. Jimmy, you're looking older.

Jimmy Whilst you, my dear, are –

Gerald Curious as to why you have cast an ageing relic of the British stage as a legendary hero.

Mick Don't run yourself down so, Gerald.

Gerald I was actually talking about you, darling. But no doubt everything will become clear?

He turns to see a nervous young man – **Damien/Alan a' Dale** *– enter, carrying a guitar.*

Gerald Well, hello.

Jimmy Damien.

Damien   I brought the er . . .

Jimmy   So I see.

Damien   Because I didn't know if you were planning on a lute. Or mandolin.

Jimmy   We'll sort that. This is Adrian and Mick. You can probably guess their parts.

Gerald   I'm Robin Hood. Gerald Maynard.

Damien   I know.

Gerald   And you are clearly rambling Sid Rumpole, the wandering minstrel.

Damien   Sorry?

Gerald   Before your time. Not to worry.

Jimmy   Okay, everybody, listen, I'm not intending we do a reading, I hate them, everybody either mumbling or giving finished Radio Four recitals before we've even started work. So a few words, any burning questions, and then you can off and get yourselves properly suited, and we kick off proper first thing.

As the others take their seats. **Damien** *sits a seat or two away from* **Sarah**.

Now our play – *The Spirit of the Man*. Don't panic, I'm not going to explain it. Part of our process is to test it for meaning, and if it doesn't have one, then to find one, hopefully. Just for openers – the life and times of Robin Hood – on the one hand it couldn't be a more traditional subject or, you know, I mean cliché even – but obviously we're taking here a somewhat different tale on the take, take on the tale.

Eddy   Man of the People, right?

Jimmy   Exactly. In our version, he's not the rich dispossessed –

Eddy   Earl of Huntington. And Locksley.

Jimmy   You been reading up?

Eddy (*shrugs*)   Bit.

Jimmy   And nor equally is Maid Marian a lady.

Gerald   Bit of a tart then, sweetheart?

Jimmy   She's not a tart, thank you, Gerald. Quite the opposite.

Sarah   She's a sexually abused serving maid.

Gerald   Upstairs, downstairs, and along the back passage?

Jimmy   Thank you, Gerald. And equally radical in our version, as some of you may have noticed, Robin Hood is not the usual young, handsome, swashbuckling hero –

Gerald   Oh really? Are you sure?

Jimmy   He's like an old-pro football player – no, not football, er, like a prizefighter past his prime, really, who's been just thrown out on the rubbish heap. No pension scheme. No support. He's had it. He's lost it. He's buggered.

Mick (*grinning*)   The casting makes perfect sense to me now. Thank you.

Gerald   Thank you, darling.

Jimmy (*warning*)   Behave, you two.

Gerald   You know we love each other.

Mick (*openly*)   We do.

Jimmy   And, taking to the forest, he meets up with others like himself. And he builds this bunch of losers into the finest fighting team – and how does he do this, he inspires them, he gives them back their self-respect, and a vision that they're going to change the world, and they fight like hell to do exactly that, and they rob the rich of their trophies and bring them home to the poor. In essence that's the tale we're telling. But I want it to stand as a metaphor for what we as theatre-makers are doing here – that we as artists, lost and bewildered perhaps, come into the dark forest of our imaginings to create a coherent and visionary team that in turn will create a vision for the wider world beyond.

Gerald   Has anybody got an aspirin?

Eddy   Are you saying that we actors here are all a bunch of losers?

Jimmy   No, no, no, well, no . . . *absolutely* no . . . *no* way no −

Gerald   I so love it when he does his Frankie Howerd.

Jimmy   I only meant in the widest metaphorical sense − just another resonance, in the same way I think the story itself will carry with it a contemporary political relevance which I don't want to underline, but hopefully it will be perceived.

Gerald   Forgive me, Jimmy, as a *Telegraph* reader you'll appreciate I know nothing of politics, but I am rather at a loss to see what particular significance a group of men in tights could have to any but a select group of my friends in Chelsea?

Eddy   It's because it's about a working-class hero who starts up a band that take on the world −

Adrian   Like the Beatles?

Eddy   What I meant was a band of fighting men.

Damien   (*nervous*)   But . . . Sorry, excuse me, it seems to me, there are actually many modern metaphors of resistance, if one thinks globally, especially around the issue of forests.

Eddy   Does Sting come into this? Can't bloody stand the man.

Mick   Forest is the clue, isn't it? I can see the politics, but there's one inspiring reference you're missing. Come on, lads, do you get it? This is Nottingham. A play about Nottingham Forest. Who else built a crap team from a forest and took it to the moon?

Eddy Brian Clough. Old Big 'Ead!

Jimmy No, no, wait, wait. This has got absolutely nothing to do with Old Big 'Ead.

Mick Pull the other leg, eh? Look at Gerald. He's the only actor in England with them eyebrows.

Gerald (*horrified*) Have I been given this part simply on the strength of facial hair?

Jimmy No, no –

Gerald I need to phone my agent. Gerald Maynard is his own man and whilst I may occasionally peck a darling on the cheek, I don't go around saying (*and the accent is good*), 'Give us a kiss, young man.'

Mick Listen to him. He's perfect.

Jimmy Hold on. Gerald, believe me, I cast you solely, totally one hundred per cent because of the strength of your acting. This Brian Clough thing – it's pure coincidence. Never occurred to me. Last thing I want is Brian Clough hovering. (*Only just holding control.*) If I was doing a play about Brian Clough, I would do a play about Brian Clough. But I am not doing a play about Brian Clough. I am doing a play about Robin Hood. Any connection this play may have with any real persons living or dead is purely coincidental. Okay? Everybody fine with that?

Silence. **Gerald** *puts up his hand.*

Jimmy Gerald?

Gerald One last question.

Jimmy Yes?

Gerald Do I wear tights?

Jimmy (*pauses*) Perhaps. Probably.

Gerald Silk or nylon?

Jimmy I'm sure we can accommodate.

Gerald   Only I'm easily irritated. (*Pause.*) 'Scuse me. I'm on a double yellow.

And he sails off. **Adrian** *follows after him. The others start to pack up.*

Jimmy   What's going on, Mick? Why's Gerald hiding behind the camp number?

Mick   Sorry. Can't tell you, mate. He'd kill me if I did.

Jimmy   I'll kill you if you don't.

Mick   I swore I wouldn't. He only told me because he was crying too much to drive. Let it go, eh? You know, Gerald's a pro. He'd hate to think his private life had affected in some way what he was doing on stage.

Jimmy   But it does. We're only human. Come on, please. We're a team. We're working together.

Mick   (*eventually*)   You ever meet Paul?

Jimmy   That his partner's name? No.

Mick   No one ever does. He hates the theatre. (*Pause.*) Hated.

Jimmy   He's dead?

Mick   And it wasn't an easy going. Don't say owt, will you? But for God's sake don't tell him. If he knew I'd betrayed him . . .

Jimmy   Secret's safe with me.

Mick   And how are things with you, Jimmy? Everything okay at home?

Pause.

Jimmy   Great. Couldn't be better.

Mick   Coming for a pint?

Jimmy   Lot to do.

Mick *goes.* **Damien** *is apparently trying to master a madrigal. He's picking out the theme of 'She Moves through the Fair'.* **Jimmy** *is staring at* **Sarah**. *She realises.*

Jimmy   Oh, sorry, I was thinking . . . I mean, is it totally impossible do you think? I mean, a man so much older than you . . . maybe it's wrong, maybe Marian could never . . . does it make any sense to you?

Sarah   (*nods*)   But she's had a very bad time with men. It may take her a while to trust . . .

Jimmy   Of course. But in the scene when they first kiss, it's not just a sympathy vote with her? There's real passion?

Sarah   I think so.

Eddy   (*butting in*)   Have we packed in for the day, or what?

Jimmy   Ye'. (*Turning back to* **Sarah**.) Perhaps we could talk about this later. I've a design meeting straight after – one tree is turning into a nightmare – but no, I feel this is more . . . you know . . . this is more important and . . . I mean, could you hang on and maybe we could get a drink away from the . . . so we can really get down to . . . and perhaps a bite to eat and . . . er . . .

Sarah   That'd be great. I really want to get sorted what's going on here.

Jimmy   So do I.

Sarah   I don't want to be a victim. You understand?

Jimmy   I don't see you as a victim at all. Quite the opposite.

She smiles and moves away to study her script.

Eddy   Do I get after-hours tuition as well?

Jimmy   You feel you need it?

Damien   Jimmy, I just wondered if –

He turns away to **Damien** *and comes face to face with* **Brian**.

Jimmy   (*cries out*)   Ah! What are you doing here?

Damien   Oh, sorry.

Jimmy   You can't just waltz into my rehearsal room.

Damien   Waltz? I thought –

Jimmy   What the hell are they going to say?

Damien   I wasn't waltzing; I –

Brian   Don't fret, sunshine. You're the only one can see me.

Jimmy   I'm so lucky. I was banging on I'd seen the back of you.

Damien   You want me to leave? Have we finished?

Brian   You would have, if word weren't you were pissing me around, young man.

Jimmy   I'm pissing you around?

Damien   No, no – no problem, honest.

Brian   Got a bone to pick.

Eddy   Do you still need me?

Jimmy   You know what you can do with your bone, don't you?

Eddy   Beg pardon?

Jimmy   Sod off!

Eddy (*dangerous*)   You what?

Jimmy   No, not you!

Damien   Me?

Jimmy   No, no – stay!

Eddy   Make your mind up.

Jimmy   What is it, what do you want, Damien?

Damien   Just a little thought . . . I wondered shouldn't I have a scene with Sarah.

Eddy   Dream on, Tommy.

Damien   Oh, I didn't mean with Sarah . . . I, er . . .

I meant Maid Marian. Everybody else has some kind of relationship, but –

Brian   How come you've got a poof playing me?

Jimmy   He's not a poof.

Eddy   Did I say he was?

Brian   He's more poof than that bloody magic dragon. I'm not having a shirt-lifter playing me.

Jimmy   He's not playing you! And he's certainly not taking the piss –

Eddy   (*pointing at* **Damien**)   You taking the piss?

Damien   'Bout what?

Eddy   If anybody's a poof –

Jimmy   Nobody's a poof!

Eddy   They all say that. And then they're searching for soap in the communal bath –

Brian   The lad has a point, you can't have a man with tape-measure eyes in your shower.

Damien   But surely I'd –

Jimmy   Just sod off, will you!

Damien   Sorry?

Jimmy   Stop saying sorry.

Brian   I'm not having it, young man.

Damien   My mother tells me off for saying it all the time –

Jimmy   Bugger your mother!

Brian   James! James! James!

Pause.

Jimmy   Sorry, Damien. I don't mean bugger *your* mother. I meant –

Brian   Perhaps we should have a shower scene where they all get to cool down.

Jimmy   NO SHOWER SCENES. NOW PISS OFF!

*Eddy and **Damien** back off.*

Jimmy   Sorry. Sorry. Terribly . . . I mean, it's just so much in my head with the set and how do you get a full tree on . . . and all the leaves . . . a nightmare. Maybe I should set the whole thing in winter, but . . . that's not your problem is it, so goodnight, lads, thank you.

They leave, both men casting a last glance at the young actress.

Jimmy   (*sighs*)   I was doing so well. I thought I was getting better, I thought . . . Okay. Nice to see you, Brian. Thank you for dropping by. It's been a long time. I am somewhat busy at the moment so –

Brian   I'm not having it. I've got nothing against back-enders, but I'm sorry, I just can't have one playing me.

Jimmy   For the last time, he is not playing you. He's playing Robin Hood.

Brian   Come on, son, them eyebrows don't grow on trees. Your Robin's only a thin allergy of me.

Jimmy   Allegory.

Brian   I knew I shouldn't have left selecting the team to you. Should have called Peter up. He'd have got somebody proper for the part. Travolta, if not De Niro. And I shouldn't have left you. You're in need of my technical help.

Silence. **Jimmy** *looks to the heavens, but there is no assistance. He tries a different tack.*

Jimmy   (*carefully*)   Mr Clough –

Brian   Brian.

Jimmy   Brian. I have enormous admiration for you and your history, amazing – what was it, two European cups –

Brian   In consecutive years with Forest, 1979, '80.

Jimmy   Brilliant, but –

Brian   League Championships and League Cup, '78, '79, '89 and '90.

Jimmy   Fantastic.

Brian   '77–'78, record forty-two straight games unbeaten in the League.

Jimmy   I take my hat off –

Brian   And then there were my own personal record as a striker –

Jimmy   Awe. That's what I feel – awe. Magnificent record. Inspirational, no question. You made Forest known throughout the world. Probably the universe. I've no doubt that even in galaxies beyond where football is played your name will be whispered in hushed tones of deep reverence.

Brian   You might just be overdoing it a bit. I say might.

Jimmy   No, take nothing away. Fantastic achievement. Michelangelo would have packed in work on the Sistine Chapel to catch one of your games.

Brian   Understandable, given that all his bloody Italian teams are nothing but cheating bastards. They bribed the ref when Forest were playing them, they cheated me out of –

Jimmy   Sorry, I didn't mean to bring up the war. But you see the point I'm making, though?

Brian   No.

Jimmy   The point is that you in the world of football are the most inspirational figure since the guy who first sewed up a pig's bladder and kicked it at his mate. But this is theatre, not football. Totally different ball park. Thank you. So bless you. And *arrivederci*. Goodbye.

Brian   If it's all the same with you, I'll just sit on the bench here. Getting interesting. Might learn a few tricks. And stop the fellow playing limp-wrist acting.

Jimmy (*sighs*)   Listen, please, Mr Clough, Brian, sir. This is a very delicate time for me. I really cannot afford to go completely and utterly mad.

Brian   It's the other way round, young man. It's what you *have* to do. Believe me.

Jimmy   Oh, ye', well, if you'll excuse me I've got a . . .

Brian   Got a what?

Jimmy   A meeting.

Brian   Oh, ye'. (*Looks at* **Sarah**.) Don't think I don't see your game.

Jimmy   I don't have a game.

Brian   Yes you do, and it's a dirty one. If I were ref I'd blow the whistle on you right now.

Jimmy   Ye', well, you're not. Sarah?

She rises. They move away. **Brian** *blows his whistle.* **Jimmy** *turns back, furious.*

Sarah   You all right?

Jimmy   Just thought I . . . fine, couldn't be better.

As he ushers her out, **Brian** *blows the whistle and points to an early shower.* **Jimmy** *stops, gives him a V-sign and goes off with* **Sarah** *in the opposite direction. Lights fade.*

Scene Three: Jimmy's Bedroom

Dark. Brian Adam's 'Everything I Do', the theme from Costner's Robin Hood, Prince of Thieves. As the music fades, **Jimmy**'*s voice is struggling to maintain the melody.*

Sarah   God, that's terrible!

Jimmy (*lightly*)   Well, I was doing my best.

She laughs. Lights. They are both in his bed (as it slides out from within the tree).

Sarah I meant the music.

Jimmy That's a relief. (*Pause.*) So is it time for the second half yet?

Sarah More champagne first.

Jimmy Your wish is my command, Lady Marian.

Sarah Don't mistake me for a lady.

Jimmy It's no mistake. (*Pours her another glass.*)

Sarah What's it like? You and I here . . . I mean, isn't this where . . .

Jimmy I caught them in flagrante delicatessen?

Sarah What does that mean?

Jimmy She was chewing on a baguette at the time.

Sarah Is everything a joke to you?

Jimmy No.

Sarah Do you still love her? (*Pause.*) Is this a kind of exorcism for you?

Jimmy Maybe. Maybe the ghosts of Bonking Past are now dissipated and gone away, and I can have my duvet back in peace. Maybe.

Sarah You didn't answer my question. Do you still love her? I shouldn't pry.

Jimmy It's just I don't know the answer. The word confuses me. Every time I look at it, it changes its meaning. Like some demented four-letter morph.

Sarah And me? Where am I in your dreams?

Jimmy (*a beat*) Can we . . . I don't want to be forward or anything, but I wouldn't mind, if you didn't mind, going for a replay . . . I mean, I get better as I get into the swing, second time will be terrific. Well, pretty impressive. Good. Quite good. Reasonable. Anyway, it'll be a bit better than the first one. Hopefully.

Sarah   The first one was really special.

Jimmy   Oh, great, because I taped it.

Sarah   I never know when you are joking or not.

Jimmy   Neither do I.

Sarah (*pause*)   Who is Maid Marian, Jimmy? I can't find the heart of her.

Jimmy   You're right. The heart of her's not there yet. I'll write you a great speech.

Sarah   How will you get to her heart?

Jimmy   I'll ask Roboin, he'll know the way.

Sarah   But does he know the way to mine? Or can you find that on your own? (*Laughing, she dives under the duvet.*)

Jimmy (*softly*)
Oh Lord, my heart, that's beating fit to break,
If Death comes now and points the path to take
I'd beg no more from him but one last wish –
I'd go in ease with Death, if I could steal
From sleeping lips, one final autumn kiss.

He turns back the cover and up pops **Brian**.

Oh, God!

Brian   Spot on, young man, but you can call me Brian in bed.

Jimmy   What the hell are you doing here?

Brian   Always on the job, sir. As you are, by the looks of it.

Jimmy   Have you been here whilst we . . . during the . . .

Brian   I closed my eyes. If it had been more than a couple of minutes I might have nodded off.

Jimmy It took longer than that.

Brian No, no, you're right. It took you half an hour to get the cork out the bottle.

Jimmy Just clear off, will you?

Brian It's just like Eric and Ernie this, isn't it? Two men man to man in bed.

Jimmy (*climbing out*) I'm not lying in bed with you discussing Morecambe and Wise. Even as a ghost, you have absolutely no right to be haunting my duvet.

Brian Now there's where you're wrong, young man. I'm here to inspire you.

Jimmy Yes, well, thank you, but I'm doing very well on my own.

Brian That's just the point, son. You are on your own.

He pulls back the sheets to reveal the empty bed. **Jimmy** *checks it out. He is stunned.*

Oh, come on, Jimmy, what is it my grandkids say nowadays – *get real.* Sorry, but come on, son, you didn't really imagine a lass like her was going snuggle up with an old misery like you, did you?

Pause.

Jimmy I did imagine.

Brian True, that's right, you're right, you did. And you've got one hell of an imagination. And that's why I'm here, so you don't lose the moment. Go for goal, son.

Jimmy What – so what . . . do you reckon that a kick in the teeth like this is supposed to be inspiring?

Brian Not half.

Jimmy How's that?

Brian Come on, son, you promised the lovely a speech. Make it a great one, eh? Get and give someowt out of all this.

Give her your *real* best shot. But keep the play on the pitch, son, not in the shower.

Silence. **Jimmy** *is locked in thought.*

Brian   Is it half-time? Is it you to go for the pies, young man?

Jimmy *nods, although to what we are not sure.* **Brian** *grins.*

Blackout.

Act Two

Scene One: Rehearsal Room – Chapel in the Forest

Inside the tree, **Maid Marian**, *kneeling in front of a small candlelit altar. She rises and moves downstage. In the shadows the other* **Merrie Men** *hover,* **Friar Tuck**, **Alan a' Dale** *and* **Little John** *softly singing a 'Gregorian' requiem chant (actually based on the song 'Such a Man'.)*

Under the greenwood tree, dappled lighting. **Gerald** *is slightly apart from the other actors.*

Sarah/Maid Marian *(singing 'Such a Man')*
Such a man
Such a man
I was proud
When he held my hand.

Such a man
Such a man
To be held in his arms
To be lifted as high
As any man can.

Such a man
As only poets dream
Such a man
Such a man.

Such a sweet gentle knight
Never keen to surrender
Fighting for freedom
With a touch all at once
So strong and so tender
I'll always remember
Such a man.

(To the audience.) He were poisoned, poisoned by a prioress. It don't matter how he come to death. Only the fact that . . .

(*Pause.*) He fired his arrow into the distant trees and we who
loved him buried him beneath the quivering feathers
unmarked but in our hearts . We stood shoulder to shoulder
sharing the tremor with the trees. Waiting for the rain to
stop, for the change, for there had to be a change, the sun
to shine, for the rainbow to break through. But it's England.
The weather don't change just for a mourner's whim. But I
looked around and there we were in Lincoln green, amidst
the golden ochre of the autumn leaves. And then I saw, just
for a moment, the simple truth. We had no need to wait for
signs from God. We were the rainbow, the rainbow that is
never seen, the rainbow all of green. (*Smiles.*) And that's all
that Robin had ever wanted us to see. We were the rainbow.
(*Smiles.*) It's so ordinary, so simple, we were not the gods of
the greenwood songs, we were just people. And he were
bad-tempered, stank to high heaven most of the time, and
never stopped scratching. And some days I swear he thought
he were God. But I miss him. And I've learnt in old age
that you still carry inside a young bride yearning for an
autumn kiss . . . You can still burn when your dry knees
crackle with age. You can still yearn. Indeed, you do not
have a choice. You can still hear the melody even when
you can no longer sing. What can I tell you about this man?
I can tell you everything. He was a man, such a man. He
was a man. Just a man.

Now unaccompanied.

Such a man, such a man
He built castles out of sand
Just a man
Just a man
But he walked like a giant
And spoke as true
As an honest man can.

Such a man
Such a man as young girls dream
Such a man
Just a man.

Silence. **Jimmy** *and the other actors stand watching her, moved. She looks shy, turns to look at* **Jimmy** *for approval. He nods.*

Jimmy (*quietly*) Ye', that's not a bad first stab at it. Sorry it took me so long to write. Okay, let's move on. Let's go to the autumn kiss sequence. Gerald? Are you ready? Gerald?

Gerald *stands stunned.*

Gerald You're intending to start the play with that scene?

Jimmy That's the idea. Then we go back in time to show what kind of man he really was.

Gerald (*softly*)
Such a man
Just a man.

Jimmy Are you all right, Gerald?

Gerald It's just. I hadn't realised . . .

Jimmy What?

Gerald That this . . . that what we are doing here, your play, that it's really a love story.

Jimmy What did you think it was?

Gerald (*eventually*) It's just opening with his funeral, it . . . I can see it's very moving but . . .

Jimmy (*finally understanding*) Oh. I'm sorry, Gerald. I didn't think . . . it simply hadn't occurred to me –

Gerald What?

Jimmy Well, your own loss. I hadn't connected that it would bring Paul and his death back in some way.

Gerald Paul?

Jimmy I should have been more –

Gerald Does the whole world know?

He stares at **Mick**.

Gerald I trusted you.

Mick *can make no answer.* **Gerald** *turns and goes before he finally breaks down.*

Jimmy   Oh, shit.

Mick   Thanks, Jimmy.

He goes after him.

Jimmy   Right, okay, we won't . . . let's not do the love scene right now. I . . . er . . . (*Totally lost.*)

Damien   Sorry, 'scuse me. I just wondered if this might be the moment, if things are still up in the air and open . . . Sarah and I, we had a small idea for a new scene, nothing really but . . . I'd been singing 'She Moved through the Fair' and we thought there might be a moment where she did move through the fair and –

Jimmy   We don't have a fair in the play.

Damien   No, sorry, yes, but I mean there could . . . You know . . . Nottingham Goose Fair. Lots of tales about Robin and Goose Fair. I just thought perhaps there could a scene where I go as a minstrel with Maid Marian to the fair and she's in disguise collecting money to ransom Richard the Lionheart, the true king, and perhaps the villain Guy of Gisbourne, you know Eddy there, who'd raped her when she was a . . . perhaps he starts throwing his weight around and I . . . or somebody like me . . . there's a big fight for her and . . .

Jimmy   (*sharply*)   I'm not big on medieval markets, Damien. Besides, I doubt we can run to a gaggle of geese.

Damien   Oh, right, yes. Sorry. It was just a thought, I hadn't worked it out or anything, just . . . sorry, sorry about the . . . Sorry. Sorry.

Jimmy   (*trying to regain control*)   Right, let's do Friar Tuck's conversion scene.

Adrian/Friar Tuck   (*edgy*)   But we haven't got Robin or Little John. Shouldn't we – ?

Jimmy   Well, improvise.

He turns round to see **Brian** *smiling at him.*

Jimmy   Oh no! All I need!

Brian   Now then, young man, how you been coping without me? Your Merrie Men don't look too cheerful. I met two of them crying on the stairs.

Jimmy   Listen, you, you . . . whatever . . . Listen, if I seem to lack the power to banish you from this realm completely, let me make one thing completely and utterly clear −

Brian   That would be a welcome change, sunshine.

Jimmy   Right. That's it. You are not the manager of this team, not even the linesman, or the man with the bucket and water, you are just a ghost, at best, just a . . . nothing, existentialist meaningless fantasy projection, right . . .

Brian   You did say clear, didn't you, young man?

As **Adrian** *approaches.*

Jimmy (*with mounting fury*)   And if you insist on hanging around, just go sit on that bench and if you cross this line, you're dead.

Brian   I am dead.

Jimmy (*marking it out*)   Just don't cross the line!

Adrian (*passing*)   Which line?

Jimmy   Not you . . . I'm just working on . . . something in my head. Can we get going. please?

Adrian   I'm not really sure that −

Jimmy   Just do it!

Adrian/Friar Tuck (*nods, singing*)
  Ego, ego, ego, sum abbas, sum abbas, sum abbas
  Cucaniensis
  Et consilium meme est cum bibulus
  Et in secta Decii voluntas mea est.

Eddy What the bloody hell is that all about?

Damien It's from *Carmina Burana*.

Eddy What, that foreign tart with the banana topping?

Damien No, no, (*Smiling.*) It's a medieval song re-set by Carl Orff. It's supposed to sound religious, but in fact it's a drunken song from an abbot. Rather apt for Friar Tuck.

Eddy How do you know all this?

Damien We sang it in the college choir.

Sarah So did we!

Eddy Oh, did we?

Jimmy (*weaving amongst them*) Shut up, will you? These are rubbish positions. You three move up here. Adrian – we can't have you starting your speech with your back to the audience, so let's have you up here. Now you lot will all come out of the mist, it'll be like a medieval version of Henry Fonda and his gang appearing through the dust in *Once Upon a Time in the West*.

Eddy/Will Scarlet There's not enough of us.

Jimmy There will be! (*To* **Adrian**.) You're drunk. So it takes a beat for you to notice them.

Adrian Ego.

Jimmy Adrian. Next speech.

Adrian/Friar Tuck Ah. Yes. A little flock. How unexpected but delightful. Is it Sunday, I'm not aware . . . alas, no communion service today, I am a mere wandering . . . wandering mendicant. Pray let me pass, my friends.

Sarah/Maid Marian (*after a silence*) Should I do Little John?

Eddy/Will Scarlet I bet he'll love that.

Jimmy Knock it off.

Eddy/Will Scarlet   No sweat. Just don't ask me to do Robin Hood.

Damien/Alan a' Dale   I'll do him.

Eddy/Will Scarlet   He'll think Christmas has come early.

Jimmy   On! On! Cue.

Adrian/Friar Tuck   Pray let me pass, my friends.

Sarah/Maid Marian (*blocking his way*)   Willingly, Father, if you are willing to make us an offering.

Adrian/Friar Tuck   An offering. Of what order?

Damien/Alan a' Dale   Your wine.

Eddy/Will Scarlet   We need wine to wash down the King's deer.

Adrian/Friar Tuck   Oh, well, if only, but alas, I'd love to share but it's sacrosanct. For the sacrament. Wafers. And now, alas, as the blessed blood of Christ, it can only be disposed of by the ordained. It is an onerous task we have to bear. (*Swigs from the flagon.*)

Sarah/Maid Marian (*raising her staff, as* **Little John**)   We too have a taste for consecrated wine.

Adrian/Friar Tuck (*suddenly affronted*)   I take this very seriously, my friend. This wine is my religion. (*Pause.*) My religion this wine. 'Tis my comforter. You can't take it away from me. It comforts me. It lies me down besides the still waters. My cup runneth over. It restoreth my soul. My rod and staff. I will fight to the death for my faith.

He kneels, clutching the wine, and starts weeping. It takes some time for others to realise something is wrong. They look to **Jimmy**.

Brian   Not much of a comedy, is it?

Jimmy *signals him to silence. He zips his mouth.* **Jimmy** *kneels by the actor.*

Adrian/Friar Tuck   I'm sorry, Jimmy. I'm so sorry. I thought I could but . . . it's like being tempted by . . . look at me, I've got the shakes . . . I could kill for a drink. I can't say these things because I believe them. This is cruel, Jimmy. Asking a man with my history to be a comic drunk. It's cruel.

Jimmy   He's not a drunk.

Adrian/Friar Tuck   But I am.

Jimmy   You're not.

Adrian/Friar Tuck   Evening. My name is Adrian Miller. I am an alcoholic. I have not touched a drop since a year last Christmas. That's the only bloody speech I can make nowadays.

Jimmy   We're about to change that.

Adrian/Friar Tuck   How?

Jimmy   You're going to be a great Friar Tuck.

Adrian/Friar Tuck   Could have been once. I can't do it without a drink.

A desperate **Jimmy** *signals for the others to turn away. The only one watching is* **Brian**.

Brian   Don't want to butt in, young man, but is he your first choice for Friar Tuck? (**Jimmy** *nods.*) Right. Then kick the bugger.

Jimmy   Doesn't work like that.

Brian   Listen, I know a thing a two about the bottle, son. Tell him to get off the deck and start passing the ball right now. Kick him! You understand I'm speaking metalogical.

Jimmy   Metaphorical.

Brian   Just tell him –

Jimmy   He's not listening.

Brian   Yell louder. If you believe in him, don't take his crap. Tell him, if you, Jimmy Potter, has picked him for the first team, he's good enough for a part in *Coronation Street* –

Jimmy   He may not feel that's the height of his professional aspiration.

Brian   Bollocks, everybody wants to play in the Premier League. (*Yelling.*) Just bloody tell him!

Jimmy (*shouting back*)   Stop yelling at me!

Adrian/Friar Tuck   I didn't say –

Jimmy   I wasn't talking to you.

Adrian/Friar Tuck   Why not?

Brian   Cos you are a cringing little shit, that's why not.

Jimmy   I can't say that.

Adrian/Friar Tuck   Say what?

Jimmy   You're a cringing little shit.

Adrian/Friar Tuck   What?

Brian   Kick and carrot, son.

Jimmy   What?

Brian   You've kicked him, now give him the carrot.

Jimmy   Carrot?

Adrian/Friar Tuck   What?

Jimmy (*desperate*)   I'm going to give you a carrot.

Adrian/Friar Tuck   Carrot?

Jimmy   Will you stop repeating everything I say! This is bloody hopeless. We don't do it like this in the theatre.

Brian and **Jimmy***'s speeches increasingly begin to overlap and increase in volume.*

Brian   Get up some steam, son. Don't pussyfoot about.
I picked you for this part, and –

Jimmy   Listen, I picked you because you can play any –

Brian   – pitch –

Jimmy   – theatre in the land!

Brian   You could be at Wembley next week –

Jimmy   You could be at Wembley, at the National –

Adrian/Friar Tuck   What?

Brian   *Coronation Street!*

Jimmy   (*as* **Brian** *blows his whistle over every F-word*)   Shut up
about the fucking street.

Brian   James, son.

Jimmy   No no, shut up. I've got this. (*With mounting fury,
fast.*) Now listen, you little spineless piece of shit, I picked
you for this fucking part, I wrote the fucking part for you,
what do you think I am a fucking prat, you are perfect for
this part, you will be fucking perfect because I am not
fucking wrong, in so far as this show goes I am God, don't
you dare fucking insult me when I'm showing you my full
faith in you as an artist. So fucking get up and stop fucking
with me now and act your fucking balls off!

Everybody is rooted to the spot. **Jimmy** *can hardly believe what he
has just said.*

Jimmy   (*to himself*)   I don't believe I fucking said that!

Brian *is equally disappointed that he missed the last one.*

Jimmy   Okay. Hm. Let's just pick the scene up from where
we left it, shall we? Ready?

Adrian/Friar Tuck (*eventually*)   I take this very seriously,
my friend. This wine is my religion. (*Pause.*) My religion this
wine. 'Tis my comforter. You can't take it away from me.
It comforts me. It lies me down besides the still waters. My

cup runneth over. It restoreth my soul. My rod and staff.
I will fight to the death for my faith.

*He rises to his feet, takes hold of his rod and twirls it around like a
samurai master. Then takes a fighting stance.*

Eddy/Will Scarlet   Well, I'm not going up against that
bugger!

Laughing, he breaks the spell and goes to hug **Adrian**. **Sarah** *and*
Damien *join in.*

Brian   Good one, son.

Jimmy *breathes a sigh of relief, but it's only a momentary respite, as
his mobile plays 'My Way'. He does his usual juggling act to find it.*

Jimmy   Have a coffee. Bloody tune. How do you change . . .
Hello. (*Pause. Suddenly still.*) Look I can't talk, I'm in the
middle of a rehearsal and . . . You want . . . what? You
want what? (*In disbelief. Struggling to overcome mounting fury.*) Well,
of course, sweetheart, I'll get you a ticket for the opening . . .
Just one? (*Pause.*) Two? (*Colder.*) Are you sure it's the gardener's
choice this, I mean, wouldn't he prefer to stay at home and
play with his sweet peas? No, no, you're right, civilised.
That's what theatre does, civilises, yes. I remember saying it,
I wish I hadn't but . . . Fine. What? Of course your things
are all still there. Well, I gave some of your lingerie to the
Jehovah's Witnesses . . . A red dress, how many you got,
two, how will I know which . . . ? Choose? . . . Yes, well,
I know it's my first night, but I . . . You want me to choose
which, oh, yes, yes, wouldn't it be simpler if he moved into
our house, after all there's two of you, you need a double
bed, I hate to think of you living in some potting shed or
has he got a tree house . . . (*Pause.*) Don't you dare hang up
on . . . .

*He realises the entire cast is watching him. He switches off the phone.
He is shaking from head to toe.*

Jimmy   Costume. Costume department. Technical problem.
(*Pause.*) No problem.

Brian   You all right, young man?

Jimmy (*whispers*)   I've lost the plot. Totally.

Brian   You're in need of a bit of rest and recuperation.

Jimmy   Oh ye', right. I've got a show to open in a couple of days.

Brian   Pre-match. Best time to take a break. We always did. 'Come fly with me, let's fly, let's fly away'.

Scene Two: A Villa in Majorca

Sudden light change. **Brian** *opens the 'doors' to reveal the terrace of a villa – a Spanish flamenco player (***Damien** *under sombrero, sunglasses and moustache) and a tiny bar. Bright sunshine. He waves his arm – the guitarist begins to play.* **Brian** *puts sunglasses on and settles in.*

Brian   Thank you, Pedro

Damien/Pedro (*in Spanish*)   Thank you, Mr Big 'Ead. (*To* **Jimmy**.) Welcome to Spain, I hope you have a pleasant stay here.

Brian   Yes, thank you, Pedro.

Jimmy   Where the hell am I now?

Brian   This was my particular pitch in Heaven. Calla Millor. Majorca. We'd come here before big games, or to celebrate after. The lads'd be down the hill in the village. Practically next door, over there, was Peter Taylor's rancho. His kids and mine'd turn golden brown together, the missuses would beehive and bouffant to their hearts' desire, and me and him, we'd do what we always did – get boozed up and talk of nought but the beautiful game. Peter – my right hand man. Right foot, to be precise. (*He chuckles to himself.*) He was one for the good life was Peter, but when he decided to jack it in, God I missed him, I tell you.

Jimmy   Do I get a pina colada whilst I'm sitting here?

Brian   Come on, this is one of them dream sequences, you know the rules. Anyway, next thing I knew, no phone call, no nothing, I hear like everybody else on the street that he's back with our old team, Derby, as manager, just down the road, and to top it, he had the bleedin' nerve to nick one of my best men, John Robertson, to go with him. Betrayal? A big word for it but . . . I don't know . . . I never spoke to him again. (*Pause.*) Only know one thing, I should have picked up the phone and just said, all right Peter you daft bogger, and I'm a daft bogger an' all, and that would have brought him running, but because I was a daft bogger I didn't, and it pains. And I'll tell you something for nothing, son – there's no kiss-and-make-up in heaven. Don't kid yourself you'll run into the shower and there they'll be, – sponge and bucket in hand, and you'll both laugh and say what a daft mistake, what a pair of prats, come on, let's make up and then go outside and play. Not an option. No, this is it, son. Wherever your studs make a mark, that's the only pitch.

Jimmy *stares at him, then nods. He dials.*

Jimmy   Oh, it's the ansaphone –

Brian   Don't hang up. Talk to the bloody thing.

Jimmy   It's me. It's . . . What do I . . . ?

Brian   Tell her . . .

Jimmy   What?

Brian   'Put on your red dress, baby.'

Jimmy   The red dress, yes, I'll tell you what . . . I'll . . . I'll drop off both dresses. And you can choose which of us, them, you love most, would want to wear . . . Yes . . . Wear for life, for the show and . . . er . . .

Brian   It's her choice.

Jimmy   Yes, it's your choice, that's fine . . . Whoever, whichever you choose, it'll be right, I'm sure it'll . . . er . . .

Brian   And after?

Jimmy   What?

Brian   Do I have to write this for you, son? After the show?

Jimmy   After the show perhaps, I don't know, perhaps we could, outside, after, we could . . . (*Desperate.*) What could we do?

Brian   Oh, bloody hell, do you want me to paint a picture, son?

Jimmy   Oh, we could just meet for a minute and . . . just you and . . . or you and him . . .

Brian (*horrified*)   What?

Jimmy   Or just you, probably on your . . . just to say hello, nothing, and, you know, I could see who, which you had chosen . . . and see if it was the same as I might have . . . and if it's not . . . that's . . . (*Lost.*) Got to go. Everybody's waiting.

He hangs up.

How was that?

Brian   Masterful. Ernie Wise would be so proud. Pedro!

A final Flamenco flourish. **Brian** *waves as the doors close on him. Sudden light change back to rehearsal room. A door slams upstage. As before, as* **Mick** *enters heading straight for* **Jimmy**.

Scene Three: Rehearsal Room

Mick   Bloody stupid.

Jimmy   I know.

Mick   Bloody stupid.

Jimmy   Are you going to keep saying that?

Mick   I might. That a problem?

Jimmy   No.

Mick   I trusted you.

Jimmy   I know.

Mick   What did you have to go and open your big gob for?

Jimmy   Bloody stupid.

Mick   Say that again.

Jimmy   I know. Sorry. Will he come back? (*Pause.*) It's not an easy time for me, Mick.

Mick   Work with it.

Jimmy   I've tried, but it keeps butting in. I can't keep it out of the way.

Mick   You're not listening to me. I said work *with* it. (*Pause.*) If you were an actor you'd understand.

Jimmy *looks at him, struggling to understand. He looks hopefully at the door as* **Adrian**, **Eddy**, **Damien** *and* **Sarah** *enter. And finally as a subdued* **Gerald**, *with no trace of campery, enters. The others look away, embarrassed, as though caught as a traditional gooseberry amongst broken lovers. Silence. Both together:*

Jimmy   I'm really sorry.

Gerald   Me first, please. I'm the actor. I make the speeches. (*Pause.*). I would like to apologise. It's a long time since I connected with a play on such a deep . . . As I say, it hadn't really occurred to me how much this play was a love story. I was not really prepared for that.

Jimmy   Nor was I.

Gerald   But you wrote it.

Jimmy   It doesn't mean I understand.

Gerald   No.

Jimmy   And is it a problem? That it's a love story?

Gerald (*pause*)   No. It's fine. I think I might be able to bring something to it.

Jimmy   Okay. Pick it up from the top of the autumn kiss.

Gerald *turns quietly to* **Sarah**. *The others now watch closely.*

Gerald/Robin   I know this is an old man's folly. What am I in thy eyes? Bits of crumpled parchment stitched together be scars. My fingers' rough brush would blood your skin, and yet it's me wha's bleedin' inside, me who stands on edge of life and death like I've never done before. Me who surrenders and thee din'st even know there'd been a war. Don't grant me mercy, nor pity more. I want nowt short of all – I want the magic cure for this endless longing. And thou mun answer, please, I beg, not from thy sympathy but from the very soul of thy desire. I can no longer hide my nakedness from thee, shivering in shadows watching from afar. The blush on th' cheek burns me. I have to risk an autumn kiss.

He kisses her. Pause. She puts her hands to her lips. Then smiles.

Gerald *turns and looks at* **Jimmy**. **Jimmy** *nods, and turns to look at* **Sarah**, *who has gone to stand by* **Damien**. **Eddy** *does not eye the young couple with a similar sympathy.* **Mick** *crosses to* **Gerald** *and puts his arm around him.*

Gerald   Need to feed the meter.

Jimmy *nods.* **Gerald** *goes.*

Jimmy (*softly*)   So now. (*Sighs.*) What do we do now? (*He looks at the young couple.*) Okay, Damien. You will go to the fair. (*Smiles.*) Geese. Let there be geese.

The rising sound of geese. Light change as the actors slowly come to life and pick up bits of costumes, swords , props, etc., for . . .

Goose Fair.

Jimmy   Damien, organise what you need.

Damien *does so.*

Jimmy *(taking up the tabor)* Right. Let's get the beat going for the dance.

As the others take up pipe and drum, **Eddy** *arrives, on 'horseback' and sings the traditional folk song, 'Nottingham Goose Fair'. Both he and the stage-horse are half in costume – he with helmet and armour, the horse still under construction. He belts out the number triumphantly. As he does so,* **Maid Marian** *wanders around collecting, then joining in a Morris-style dance with* **Adrian** *until, exhausted from spinning, he falls to the ground.*

Eddy/Guy of Gisbourne
Let people talk of times so hard, of starving and the like
They'll find if to the fair they'll come they are mistaken quite.
Here they may cram with beef and ham till their belly's like a drum
And swig such ale that ne'er can fail to send them rolling home.
Then haste away, make no delay, to Nottingham repair
And if you're fond of fun and glee, you'll find it at the fair.
When evening draws the curtain and bids the day goodbye
Why then unto the alehouses the lads and lasses fly
And there you'll find unto your mind, what ne'er was known to fail
The joy-inspiring tankard, boys, of far-famed Nottingham ale.
Then haste away, make no delay, to Nottingham repair
And if you're fond of fun and glee, you'll find it at the fair
And if you're fond of fun and glee, you'll find it at the fair.

Jimmy Yes, well, that's absolutely . . . *(Nods.)* Yes. No.

Eddy What do you mean, 'No'?

Jimmy There's something . . . . The dance . . . I don't know that I can cope with Morris dancing. You see them coming towards you on a summer's day with their bells and their . . . and you just head for the nearest pub, don't you? No, sorry, it's not that you are not doing . . . because you are . . . But, no . . . cut the dance.

Eddy Still got the song, though.

Jimmy Oh, yes, the song. Yes, no, sorry. Sorry, it's a song to dance to, isn't it, and once there's no dancing . . . (*Sighs.*) No point to the song.

Eddy You can't go cutting it. It sets the scene. It tells people we're at a fair. Without that, they could be anywhere.

Damien Excuse me, sorry, don't want to butt in but . . . there is actually another song we could use that sets up not just the fair but really focuses on Marian, the central character here −

Eddy This is Guy of Gisebourne's scene, mate.

Damien Well, yes, of course, in one way, but −

Jimmy What song?

Damien 'She Moves through the Fair'. It's a love song.

Jimmy We're running out of time. You think we can slot it in?

Damien Well, we've actually been rehearsing . . . Sarah and I . . . not rehearsing . . . playing . . . the two of us . . .

Jimmy Let's give it a try.

Eddy But I don't know it.

Jimmy You don't sing it. It's a song for the minstrel.

Damien Sorry.

Eddy Sorry!

Jimmy Let's go.

Eddy So what do I now? Just gallop in like the Lone Ranger and say nothing?

Jimmy No. No, of course not. (*Pause.*) Too big an

entrance. Damien's right – it would take the focus away from their song.

Eddy So what are you saying?

Jimmy   Cut the horse, Eddy.

Silence.

Eddy   Cut the horse? Cut my horse? You can't do that.

The groom pulls the horse off backwards

How the bloody hell am I to get on stage?

Jimmy   I don't know. (*To himself.*) Catch a bus. (*To everyone.*) Come on, let's get moving.

Eddy (*to **Damien**, as he disappears*)   This is your fault, you little twat.

Eddy *glares at **Damien** and rides off. **Damien** begins to sing as a hooded **Maid Marian** goes collecting, before finally joining in the song.*

Damien/Alan a' Dale (*sings 'She Moves through the Fair'*)

> My young love said to me
> My mother won't mind
> And my father won't slight you
> For your lack of kind.
>
> She stepped away from me
> And this she did say
> It will not be long love
> Till our wedding day
>
> She stepped away from me
> And moved through the fair
> And fondly I watched her
> Move here and move there.
>
> And she went her way homeward
> With one star awake
> As the swan in the evening
> Moved over a lake.

Maid Marian *carries a sack for collecting money and, in various postures as multi-characters,* **Adrian** *and* **Mick** *make the widow's mite offering, until she comes face to face with the knight* **Guy of Gisbourne**. *During this* **Brian** *hovers.*

Eddy/Guy of Gisbourne   These offerings you are collecting, wench, what import have they?

Sarah/Maid Marian   To ransom a king from betrayal.

Eddy/Guy of Gisbourne   Then let me take the weight from your tender frame. For we are well met. I am Lord Guy of Gisbourne, appointed by Prince John to raise taxes to exactly this effect. Hand me your bounty.

Damien/Alan a' Dale   That is impossible, sire.

Eddy/Guy of Gisbourne   Who gave permit for this whelp to speak?

He tries to snatch the bag from **Maid Marian**. **Alan a' Dale** *steps in between.*

Eddy/Guy of Gisbourne   Out of my way, or forthwith I'll smash your fucking face in!

Jimmy   It would be nice if you could just make an occasional gesture to the words I've actually written!

Eddy/Guy of Gisbourne   I did say forthwith. Look, I'm trying to get to the character, but the words don't help. They don't work. They've got no balls to them.

Jimmy   Just give them a chance, will you? His line is dependent on your cue.

Brian (*appears from the shadows*)   Pass the ball, you dickhead.

Jimmy   Oh no.

Brian   Just watching, young man. Have no fear.

Eddy/Guy of Gisbourne   Step aside. Or prepare your final prayer.

Sarah/Maid Marian   Alan, no.

Damien/Alan a' Dale   I'm ready with the prayer, my lord.

Eddy/Guy of Gisbourne   You're taxing my patience, my boy. And taxing is my task, I'll have no other play my part. We can ill afford to have the world turned upside down. Come, dance and play for me. (*Cuts the air around the boy with his sword.*) Dance, you fool, dance.

Damien/Alan a' Dale   I'm not a fool, sir.

Sarah/Maid Marian   Dance, please, Alan. Dance for me.

Eddy/Guy of Gisbourne   Soon you'll have no legs to play.

The boy parries with his lute, but has one advantage over the heavily armoured knight – mobility – darting in and out, under his arm, through his legs. **Brian** *is really enjoying it, but* **Guy** *is getting more and more frustrated.*

Brian   Come on, son, he's a big bugger, but use his bulk against him. Make him dizzy. That's it. Bloody hell, the kid's fast, he's like Archie Gemmill!

Jimmy   Behave.

Brian   This would be ace in slow motion, young man. Come on. Come on. Now get in the penalty area. Foot on the ball, son.

The confused **Guy**, *spinning round, suddenly comes face to face with* **Alan a' Dale** *– a moment's pause as he raises his sword.*

Brian   Now go for goal!

And **Alan a' Dale** *reaches up, pulls down the man's helmet over his eyes, and then kicks* **Guy** *with deadly accuracy in the penalty area. He goes down like the fall of the Tower of Babel.* **Alan a' Dale** *risks a foot on the man's chest and a victory salute. He's laughing. The others applaud.*

Jimmy   Brilliant. Well done. Okay –

But victory is short-lived. **Guy** *grabs his foot and sends him spinning backwards, and then leaps onto him almost crushing the lad under his weight.*

Eddy/Guy of Gisbourne   I'll crush your fucking balls, you little wanker!

A moment's panic as they all realise this is not part of the rehearsal. **Mick** *and* **Adrian** *move in to drag* **Guy** *off.* **Sarah** *rushes up to comfort the boy.*

Jimmy   What the hell are you doing, Eddy?

Eddy (*held tight by* **Mick**)   Get off me!

Sarah (*to* **Damien**)   Are you all right?

He groans. She ministers to the groaning boy.

Eddy   Oh, come on, come on. Bloody hell, I hardly touched him. He's putting it on.

Jimmy   What are you playing at?

Eddy   Well, you wanted it to look real, didn't you?

Brian   Red card. Bench the bugger. No question.

Eddy   I was just improvising. Didn't know he was such a ponce.

Jimmy   Get out.

Eddy   Oh, come on. He's just playing up for sympathy.

Jimmy   Get out now!

Mick *practically throws him against the back wall.*

Eddy   Bloody stupid.

Mick *keeps him blocked up there as he paces like a caged tiger. Finally, he returns to his weights, and works off his fury in a fit of exercise.* **Jimmy** *moves in on* **Damien***, passing by* **Brian***.*

Adrian   Should I get the first aid?

Brian   Should always have a sponge and bucket handy.

Jimmy   See how he is first.

Adrian   I hope he's all right.

Brian   Pray it's not his cruciate ligament.

Jimmy (*sharply*)   What are you, some angel of bloody doom?

Adrian (*shocked*)   I didn't mean –

Brian   Give him brandy.

Jimmy   Do we need a brandy!

Adrian   No, I don't, honest. It never occurred to me. I'm fine.

Jimmy   Who's talking about you?

Adrian   What?

Brian   Take no notice, young man. He's barking.

Jimmy (*pushing past him*)   How's he going?

Sarah   Don't think there's anything broken.

Damien (*confused*)   Sorry. I was supposed to win, wasn't I?

Sarah   You did win.

Damien   Did I?

Sarah   No doubt.

Jimmy   Are you sure you're going to be all right?

Damien (*nods*)   Just might mean . . . putting all the songs in a higher key.

*As **Adrian** carefully brings him to his feet:*

Jimmy   Just get him checked out, okay? And don't forget the brandy.

Adrian   Why you going on about it? I'm fine.

Jimmy   Break now. We'll do the ending next.

As they leave:

Eddy.

Mick *backs off guard duty.* **Eddy** *sinks finally onto the bench.* **Brian** *moves up and sits by him.*

Brian   Right bloody place for you an' all. On the bench.
If it were up to me . . .

Jimmy   Shurrup!

Eddy   Didn't say anything.

Jimmy   Thanks, Mick.

He sits on the other side. **Mick** *goes.*

Jimmy   What do you think I should do, Eddy?

Eddy   'Bout what?

Jimmy   Oh, come on, you could have killed the lad.

Eddy   Bit of rough and tumble, that's all. Comes with the
job.

Jimmy   You lost it completely.

Eddy   I've never lost it.

Brian   Red card. No question, ref. Put him on the transfer
list, I would.

Jimmy   Shurrup!

Eddy   Don't tell me to fucking shurrup. Nobody tells me to
shurrup –

Jimmy   Oh, just shurrup you, anyway! I'm sick to the
teeth with. . . . What's got into you? Is it the girl? Are you
jealous?

Eddy   What? Of him? I could snap him in two any time
I fancied.

Jimmy   That's guaranteed to win you fair lady.

Eddy   She's a stuck-up little bitch. I fancied her at first
but . . . no, not my cup of tea.

Jimmy   So why you taking it out on the lad?

Eddy   I'm not. (*Pause.*) I'm taking it out on you.

Jimmy   Me?

Eddy Ye', you, Mister hit-them-with-the truth-no-matter-what. Take no prisoners. Tell it like it is. Crap.

Jimmy You're going to have to let me in here, Eddy. You're a really good actor but I can't . . . You've got to give me something or I'm going to have to replace you late as it is, you know that. I can't a risk a madman with a sword out there.

Eddy Be a blessing.

Jimmy Why would it?

Eddy You think I'm thick as two planks, but I'm not. And I do happen to believe there's more to the world than kissing the arse . . . . Oh, what's the point?

Jimmy No, come on, Eddy. Go for it. Spit it out.

Eddy I've seen some of your plays. They're what made me want to do this daft bleeding job in first place. Auditioned for some of them an' all. I thought they were bloody great They said sommat about the real world, about my world. They had meaning. I was through the window and up to the moon when I got this.

Jimmy But I've betrayed you in some way?

Eddy What pisses me off is, I'm the only one who's clocked what you're doing.

Jimmy What am I doing?

Eddy The ending. You said it were open, but it never was, was it? Whatever we do, it always comes back to the same thing. Something to make your first night darlings feel caring, heart-in-the-right-place bollocks without one of them having to lift a bloody finger. Well, that may be great for your luvvy-luvvy champers brigade, but I tell you this, mate, it means bugger all to people like me.

Jimmy You denying it's true? What do you want, Eddy, should we finish with a knees-up with the Merrie Men all pissed on Shippoes ale and lining up for a piece of a Bakewell tart?

Eddy   You do think I'm thick. I'm not saying where you take us finally is wrong, no, that's true, that's what I read an' all, that's important, but . . . you can't stop there . . . (*Shakes his head.*) It's not right. It's wrong.

Jimmy   So what should I do?

Eddy   I don't know, I'm not the writer. I just know you can't end there. We've got to go beyond that.

Jimmy   There is no beyond. Lost in the forest. End of story.

Eddy   Robin would never have done that, not in a million years.

Brian   Done what? What's Psycho here going on about?

Jimmy *puts up a hand for silence.*

Eddy (*eventually*)   So I'm on my way or what?

Brian   Too bleedin' –

Jimmy   Don't say anything.

Eddy   I won't. I've said my piece.

Jimmy (*eventually*)   Do you want to go on?

Eddy   This is my first job in yonks. I walk and it's my last, in't it? You've got me by the short and curlies. And that's what makes me see red.

Brian   So you bloody should, young man. I'd be waving one in front of your face right now.

Jimmy (*eventually*)   Yellow.

Eddy   What?

Jimmy   Yellow card, Eddy. Be warned.

Eddy *nods, and then goes.*

Brian   You're bonkers. I'd have had him on free transfer before he could polish his balls.

Jimmy (*quietly*)   And this time, Brian, this time, you'd have been wrong.

Brian   So what are you going to do?

Jimmy   I'm going to do it my way!

Brian *does a double-take at this, as* **Jimmy** *moves to his tech table downstage.*

Jimmy (*through Tannoy link*)   Right, everybody. Stand by, ready to tech the final scene.

Scene Four: The World Turned Upside Down

Light change. A giant of a man, **Stranger** (*played by* **Mick**), *shrouded in a thick mantle. The sound of* **Robin***'s horn in the distance. The voice of* **Maid Marian** *and* **Alan a' Dale** *singing a translation of Chevalier's 'Mult Estes Guariz'.*

Our Lord will guide
Each ev'ry day
To lead us on to victory.

Our Lord will guide
Each ev'ry night
We fight for light against the blind.

Our Lord will guide
Each every day
And bring us back with banners high

(*Sung as a round.*)

You must not doubt salvation's yours
In raising swords for Richard's cause.

Maid Marian *appears as a shadowy shape. Other voices and shapes* (**Alan a' Dale**, **Will Scarlet**, **Friar Tuck**) *around her.*

Mick/Stranger
What are you? What is this maid?
And you, this man of God?

Why go you forth with naked blade?
Are you real? Are you true?
Can you survive the light of day
Or are you death's enchanting spirits?

They circle the **Stranger***. They take a step towards him. He draws his sword and sweeps a circle around him.*

Mick/Stranger (*drawing his sword*)
Do not hinder me upon my path. Make way.
I will tread this English land,
Like any Englishman should do,
Sure of foot, head held high, above all free.

Eddy/Will Scarlet
But it needs King Richard's crown
To shine on this our shore,
To help the poor,
To live as you would have them do.

Gerald/Robin Hood
But, sir, to make your dream come true,
We must see the very world itself turned upside down.

He holds a rope, and as he slides off the tree the other noosed end snaps up over the **Stranger***'s feet, and he ends up flying upside down into the air, where he twists and turns flaying around with his sword.* **Will Scarlet** *takes hold of the rope.* **Robin** *sits down quietly underneath him with* **Maid Marian***. As the* **Stranger** *finally gives up:*

Gerald/Robin Hood (*simply*)   I have a truly common dream. The world turned upside down. Our lords will scatter bounty from their bellies to the poor.

Friar Tuck *sticks the man in the stomach with his sword. A moment's stillness, then a torrent of gold coins unleashes from his hidden money belt, and* **Maid Marian** *catches it with expert ease in her lap.*

Gerald/Robin Hood   Pardon this unexpected levy. But until our true King's home again, them that know the most of tax are forced to taxing measures. To console, half we return to the poor and half goes to the ransom for our King.

Mick/Stranger   Is that the truth?

Gerald/Robin Hood   The naked truth, as naked as the kids that walk barefoot our city streets.

Mick/Stranger   Then I begrudge not the moiety for them but cannot willingly surrender money for this King.

Gerald/Robin Hood   Sir, we seek to treat you as an honoured guest but if you malign –

Mick/Stranger   Ransom not the King!

Gerald/Robin Hood   I can but admire, even in a foe, a man who, with the blood still rushing to his brain, dares tell his captors what they must and must not do.

Mick/Stranger   I have had long practice keeping courage in dark captivity.

Robin *and the others have now risen to stare at him.*

Mick/King Richard   Let me down, Robin Hood.

Gerald/Robin Hood   You know me?

Mick/King Richard   I have sought thee out. I am thy destiny. Save the widow's mite, Robin. There is no point in ransoming the very king who hangs in front of you.

A rapid series of double-takes.

Gerald/Robin Hood (*realising*)   Oh, Lord.

Mick/King Richard   Lord indeed.

Robin *rises, kneels, rises, kneels again. The others, stunned, follow suit.*

Mick/King Richard   My loyal friends, I'm much moved. But might it be possible to have my feet back upon the ground?

Gerald/Robin Hood (*as they hastily bring him down*)   My Lord, we meant no harm.

Mick/King Richard (*laughing*)   None taken, Robin. How could I?

Gerald/Robin Hood   Then honour us and let us show you the true welcome of the forest.

As **Richard** *throws away his mantle to reveal his crusader's red cross:*

Mick/King Richard   I thank you. But I must beg you at first light to leave this place. I need each and every maid and man to help me purge this poisoned land. But first our true Lord must be restored to his home land. What can we be set upon this earth for, but to redeem Jerusalem for Jesus? Follow your king on the Holiest of Holy Crusades! Hurrah! Hurrah! Hurrah!

The others cheer and end with a rousing 'Hurrah!' They turn to exit to the Chevalier marching music as an exhausted **Maid Marian** *walks forward.*

Jimmy (*on Tannoy*)   Hold it. Lighting cue's late, and sound needs to come in much louder. Reset please.

Brian *pops up behind* **Jimmy***.*

Brian   Now then, young man.

Jimmy *shudders.*

Brian   You're not going to end like that are you? The King comes back, waves his wand, and all's right with the world? No, no, I'm the last in line to say monarchy works miracles. I had the Queen lay hands on me once but it didn't cure my bad back. You're got to come up with something with a bit more bite. Eh, wasn't he a Frenchie? Another bloody foreign manager? Tell you what – why don't you leave him hanging upside down and do what the Frogs would do – eat his horse!

Jimmy (*sharply*)   It's not the end!

Brian   Oh, sorry, sunshine.

Jimmy   Okay. Take it from 'But first our true lord'.

The action resumes.

Mick/King Richard   But first our true Lord must be restored to his home land. What can we be set upon this earth for but to redeem Jerusalem for Jesus? Follow your king on the Holiest of Holy Crusades! Hurrah! Hurrah! Hurrah!

*Richard and the **Merrie Men** exit to music as an exhausted **Maid Marian** walks forward.*

Maid Marian   The men went. The years passed as the taxes to pay for distant drums broke the people's back. Is this what God asks for, is this our sacrifice? The men will return in victory. They will return, singing, marching under an ever-present rainbow. They must. The suffering has no meaning else. (*Pause.*) And it is true. In part. They did return.

She turns to see a line of exhausted and wounded soldiers, as they enter from the burnt-out inners of a rotting tree. A distant mouth organ plays the last post.

Sarah/Maid Marian   Robin! Is it you?

Gerald/Robin Hood   Is this England? Is this the heart? Are there lions in this forest? Once there were a lion here. Once I followed its roar, I ran joyous as it led us to Jerusalem. Jerusalem. It was not how we imagined it to be.

The world slowly shifts, with projections of a burn out Middle Eastern town – it could be Fallujah, Gaza, Kabul. No people, but ripped apart buildings.

Gerald/Robin Hood   The lion taught us how to feed as a pack. The pride. The pride of England. What we did . . . what . . . in the name of . . . We were betrayed. I betrayed my men by singing hymns that said we could change the world, I betrayed them with hope. It's the innocent lamb that draws the lion to feed.

Sarah/Maid Marian (*moving forward to hold him*)   Oh, Robin.

Gerald/Robin Hood (*gestures her to stop*)   You can't hold me, my love. We're all dead men here. Dead men, returning on a freezing wind to lick our wounds, and bury our souls amongst the autumn leaves. And to whisper in that wind, – hide yourself, hide yourself, my friends. Hide your face from one another lest you leave the trace of desire and hope. Only the fool fights. Hide. (*Turns to* **Little John.**) My bow!

Little John *hands it to him, and* **Robin** *takes his bow and snaps it in two. It echoes through the forest. He sinks to the ground. Around him even his men look stunned. The curtain falls.*

Jimmy (*pleased, into Tannoy*)   Thank you. Well done, everybody. Okay. Curtain up in two hours. Take a break. Shower. And no shagging!

He turns round to see a shape trying to fight its way through the curtain. Eventually **Brian** *sticks his head through –*

Brian   Well, that worn't a lorra lorra laughs, young man.

Jimmy   I never said I was writing a comedy.

Brian   No, but now that Ernie's retired, some of us had hoped.

Jimmy   Exactly. Hope. There's the trap. Our lords and masters, they always tempt us with hope, lead us on, and then take us to the cleaners along with the jockstraps. The essential human condition isn't faith, hope and charity, it's lying, deception, betrayal.

Brian   Oh, don't start that bollocks again. Jimmy. You can't end the play like that. Your Psycho were right. I should have listened.

Jimmy   You told me to stick to my guns.

Brian   Aye, but I didn't know which way they were pointing. Fair enough, son, name of the game, get the ball in the net, but not your own. Come, give us a break, young man, I'm supposed to be inspiring you. If the angels get a shufty at this, I won't even get sent out for Sunday football. Come on, you can't end like that.

Jimmy   That's the way life is. I'm not changing it.

Brian (*Pause*)   Hang on. What's up here? Lady in red given you the elbow? Or not phoned you back, is that it? Don't tell me this is all because a woman decided you weren't her idea of a buttered scone.

Jimmy   To love is human, to betray divine.

Brian   Well, that's going to pack them in, son. I can see the badges and the T-shirts now.

Jimmy   I don't care.

Brian   Well, I do. Your Eddy were right, you can't have Robin Hood snapping his bow in half and giving up the fight. That'd be like me putting a nail in a football. It don't make no sense. I'm not letting you do this, son. Not letting you let *them* down neither. I wasn't sent here just for you – I was called to inspire the whole team.

Jimmy   What you going to do – get them to sing 'I Did It My Way' for the finale?

Brian   Eh, that's not such a bad idea.

Jimmy   Here's the news, gaffer. You're not real. You don't exist.

Brian (*pauses*)   You think Brian Clough is going to let a little thing like that bother him?

Jimmy   You're too late. It's the opening night.

Brian   And I've heard them say you never go to first nights . . .

Jimmy   That's right.

Brian   Well, watch the last ten minutes tonight, sunshine! Game in't over till the final whistle.

He disappears into the darkness. **Jimmy** *looks at his mobile, and then throws it high up into the tree. Sudden light change.*

Scene Five: Opening Night – The Forest

Robin Hood *stands as before, in front of* **Maid Marian**, *with his shadowy soldiers beyond. As she reaches out to him:*

Gerald/Robin Hood (*gestures her to stop*)   You can't hold me, my love. We're all dead men here.

Dead men, returning on a freezing wind to lick our wounds, and bury our souls amongst the autumn leaves. And to whisper in that wind – hide yourself, hide yourself, my friends. Hide your face from one another lest you leave the trace of desire and hope. Only the fool fights. Hide.

He turns to **Little John**

Gerald/Robin Hood   My bow!

Robin *stands, lost in thought. He turns, as* **Little John** *makes to offer him his bow. He stares at the projection he is trapped in. The others are becoming confused, not knowing what to do in the situation.*

Mick/Little John   Robin, your bow is here.

He shakes his head. It's as though he's listening to someone else.

Sarah/Maid Marian   Come rest, my love.

Gerald/Robin Hood (*suddenly angry*)   No! No!

He waves his arm like a demented Lear against the storm.

Gerald/Robin Hood   NO!

As **Friar Tuck** *tries to move to support him:*

Adrian/Friar Tuck   My old friend, let me . . .

Gerald/Robin Hood   Don't touch me!

Friar Tuck *backs away, mumbling. For the first time.* **Gerald** *now sounds like Brian Clough.*

Gerald/Robin Hood   Steady. Foot on the ball. You're in the corner, Robin. They think it's all over . . . you're trapped? No.

Mick/Little John (*covering*)   Robin had a terrible fever, so many wiped out, like flies to wanton –

Gerald/Robin Hood   No! Listen, listen, nothing else matters but this moment. Understand! We are not many. We are one. Trust me. We are one.

Silence.

Robin   We *were* betrayed. Even to death. But it's not over yet. Even dead men – no, most of all dead men – burn with anger. We must rise up, spirits in the night, and reveal our true face, and stare into the eyes of the living and search out the trace of courage and desire. Where e'er it flickers at the corner of a mouth, the curtain of an eye. The game is not over. We must never, dead or alive, give up the fight. Love may be betrayed, but at heart . . . Don't wait for kings to roar like lions. Bring me my bow.

Little John *steps forward.* **Robin** *turns away from him and to* **Alan a' Dale**.

Gerald/Robin Hood (*insistent*)   Young man, listen to me young man –

Bring me my bow
Bring me my bow . . . (*Waves at him to play the lute.*)
Of burning gold. (*Singing brokenly, exhausted.*)
Bring me my bow of burning gold . . .

Friar Tuck *nudges* **Alan a' Dale** *into play – and begins to sing with him, as* **Little John** *steadies his old friend and gives him his bow.*

Bring me my bow of burning gold,
Bring me my arrows of desire

And the others join in, as **Robin** *turns to* **Will Scarlet**, *who finally hands him an arrow and joins in with the song.*

Bring me my bow of burning gold,
Bring me my arrows of desire,
Bring me my spear! Oh, clouds unfold,
Bring me my chariot of fire.

I will not cease from mental fight
Nor shall my sword sleep in my hand,
Till we have built Jerusalem
In England's green and pleasant land.

Gerald/Robin Hood (*spoken*)   Till we have built Jerusalem
in England's green and pleasant land.

He raises his bow for the last time and fires.

Blackout.

The sound of the arrow flying through the air to thwack into a tree (the opening sound of the sixties TV series). The sound reverberates through the building.

Epilogue: Outside the Theatre

Opening night. Posters proclaiming THE SPIRIT OF THE MAN. *Cold. Dark. Sounds of first-night party from inside.* **Jimmy** *is gazing up at the sky.* **Gerald** *comes out.*

Gerald Party's started, Jimmy.

Jimmy I'm just waiting for someone. (*Pause.*) A friend. Friends.

Gerald Only . . . everybody's expecting you, you know, to . . .

Jimmy I'll be in in a minute.

Gerald (*pause*) Listen, I . . . I just wanted to say I'm so sorry.

Jimmy What for?

Gerald The ending. I don't know what possessed me. You know me, Jimmy. I'm a fervent text man. Always stick to the script. So what happened tonight? Same sentence structure, punctuation, and then suddenly all was different, all was thrown into jeopardy. (*Pause.*) Paul, my partner, I don't think you ever met him. When he passed away . . . it was not an easy parting. He did not go gentle into the night. (*Pause.*) The last scene. (*Pause.*) I suddenly could not let Robin go in such a way. It was as though someone was whispering to me, as though, for the first time ever I might say, I was being prompted from the wings.

Jimmy (*quietly*) And who was it?

Gerald I don't know. Paul? Robin Hood himself? (*Pause.*) Or the real heart of your piece? (*Pause.*) There may not be a meaning to life, Jimmy. But it's only common humanity to act as though there is. Have I ruined your play for you?

Jimmy It's not mine, Gerald. We made it together. You just ran with the play and then headed in the last-minute goal.

Gerald   So the score still stands?

Jimmy   *Proudly.*

Adrian *and* **Mick** *appear.*

Mick   Everything okay out here?

Jimmy   Fine.

Gerald   Do you want me to save you a vol-au-vent? You know what actors are like. Vultures with free food.

Jimmy   Thank you.

Mick   Cheers, Jimmy. Come on, you old bugger. Don't want you catching something nasty.

Gerald   Chance would be a fine thing.

Mick *puts an arm around him, and they enter the theatre together.*

Adrian   I did it.

Jimmy (*a beat*)   How's the orange juice?

Adrian   Full of vitamin C. Foul. Has it turned out like you imagined?

Jimmy   I can't answer that. I really can't.

Sarah *enters, holding a glass.* **Adrian** *grins at her and goes in.*

Sarah   I brought you a glass of champagne.

Jimmy   Thank you.

Sarah   I tried to steal you a bottle. But they spotted me.

Jimmy   This is provincial rep. One bottle for every ten people. You were wonderful. Thank you.

Sarah   Thanks for everything. Oh, I did wonder, I mean you didn't come backstage?

Jimmy   I never do. It's time for the world to enter, for family and friends.

Sarah   Aren't we friends?

Silence. **Damien** *appears. He doesn't realise* **Jimmy** *is there.*

Damien   Sarah, some of the crew are going dancing later, shall we – Oh, sorry, am I –

Jimmy   Not at all.

Damien   No, sorry, I –

Jimmy   If you say that word again, I'll get your mam to work you over. Now go on, clear off, the pair of you. I'll be a minute. I have to meet someone.

As the two turn to leave, they meet **Eddy** *with a plate piled with food. A beat.* **Eddy** *nods at them. They nod back and exit. He approaches* **Jimmy***. It's a shy meeting.*

Eddy (*eventually*)   Meat? Venison. And wild boar. Killed them meself with my own bare hands. In the interval.

Jimmy   Glad to see you're not wasting your time here.

Eddy   Not at all. And I tried to get you a Bakewell tart, but . . .

Jimmy   She left early? (*Smiles.*) Story of my life.

Silence.

Eddy   The ending. Ghosts fighting back. (*Nods.*) Cracker. You want mustard?

Jimmy *shakes his head.* **Eddy** *turns to go.*

Jimmy   Eddy. Thank you.

Eddy   No problem.

Jimmy   No, listen to me. Thank you.

A pause. **Eddy** *turns and leaves. As he goes back inside, he passes* **Brian***, who gives him a nod.* **Jimmy** *doesn't have to turn to see him, as* **Brian** *sits by his side.*

Brian   When colour first came out on our tellies, you might recall, you 'ad a control thingy and you could make it

burn up with brilliant reds and yellows or fade it down to
dirty shades of grey. But through the eighties and nineties
some buggers took over the controls, started fiddling with the
knobs, and step by step everything, including football, lost its
colour and for all the yelling and shouting it all became a
grey game. More goings on off than on the pitch. When you
heard players were good at playing both ends it meant in
the bedroom, not in the park. And you started to forget
what had happened once upon a time, to forget you'd ever
been there, ever seen anything different. (*Pause.*) 1979.
Forest's first European Cup Final against the Swedish
champs, Malmö, at the Munich Stadium. John Robertson,
the man the papers called the *scruff*, but he's taken the ball
right up to their corner flag and they're all over him, he's
trapped, buggered, but it's then he stops for a mo, puts his
foot on the ball, and suddenly we know, all of us, friend and
foe, exactly at the same sec that he does, that something's
going to change, something luvverly is going to be born.
And he hardly needs to look up but lifts the ball, and it flies,
and it was slow motion as the rest of our team apparently
ran in different directions, pulling their lot away from its
flight, and then floating in above them, as if from another
world, the first English million-pound signing, Trevor
Francis, he's just sprouted wings, and the ball and him we
all know are destined for each other like Romeo and Juliet,
destined for one final kiss – and what a smacker it was –
smack into the back of the net. There's no reaction, no one
moves, just a sigh from the whole planet, even the losing
team sighs – shit, beautiful, inspired, the game had changed.
It wasn't just it was the winning goal, though that helped, it
was . . . (*Shakes his head. Pause.*) And I'll tell you something,
Jimmy, they called me Old Big 'Ead, and sure I shouted
enough that I had to do it my way, but my way was the
team. I didn't kick that goal in. That were done by a lad who
looked like he'd been pulled through a hedge backwards,
and another you could hardly get hold of for Brylcreem,
and the rest of the lads. Moving in different directions, but
moving as one. One dream. And that's what I lived for –
not the applause, not the fame or the fortune, nor the

chanting of your name when you come out on the pitch –
though they're better than a kick in the penalty box – but . . .
you get what I'm saying . . . .

Jimmy   The 'luvverly' game.

Brian *stands up to leave.* **Jimmy** *rises. The men stand rather
clumsily together.*

Brian   Best be off. Don't want to play gooseberry.

Jimmy   Do you think she'll turn up?

Brian   Not my field.

Jimmy   No.

Brian   Oh, come on, give us a kiss, young man.

And he hugs him somewhat clumsily.

Jimmy (*surprised*)   I can feel that.

Brian   Should bloody hope so.

And as **Jimmy** *turns to look at* **Brian**, *he is suddenly on the bank
of the Trent, with the river and on the farthest shore the back of the
Forest stadium.* **Brian** *is walking across the river.*

Jimmy   Brian. Brian!

Brian (*turns*)   What?

Jimmy   You're walking on water.

Brian   Well, don't look so surprised, young man.

He turns away.

Jimmy (*calling*)   Brian.

Brian   Aye?

Jimmy   I can't really believe I'm saying this, but . . .
I need a big finish, don't want to go out on a dying fall.

Brian   I don't want no come-back. Are you sure?

Jimmy *gives a big thumbs-up.*

Brian *begins to sing 'My Way', slowly speaking the words at first, then gradually moving into his version of 'singing'.*

As he sings, the 'stadium' opens up and he is joined by his backing group – his **Merrie Men***, now in football shirts. And above, now with her wings, the* **Perfect Little Angel***. Downstage, unnoticed by* **Jimmy***, a* **Woman in Red** *enters, and sits quietly, back to the audience.*

And **Jimmy** *finally joins in on the last line.*

Yes, it was my way.

He turns round to see the **Woman in Red***. A beat.*

Blackout.